Dark World

Into the Shadows with the Lead Investigator
of The Ghost Adventures Crew

Zak Bagans

Kelly Crigger

Las Vegas

First Published in 2011 by Victory Belt Publishing.

ISBN 13: 978-1-936608-85-0

This book is for educational purposes. The publisher and author of this book are not responsible in any manner whatsoever for any adverse effects arising directly or indirectly as a result of the information provided in this book. If not practiced safely and with caution, paranormal investigations can be hazardous to your health.

Printed in The United States

Dedication

To all the spirits I have communicated with.
They have changed my life
and my look on the afterlife.

Table of Contents

Foreword

here is arguably no topic in human history that incites as much contemptuous disbelief and passionate dedication as the existence of life after death. As humans, it is our natural instinct to belittle what we don't understand, and then follow with statements of derision and ridicule. Even mentioning that ghosts might exist can cause instant damnation and persecution among the religiously devoted and staunchly pragmatic, which causes many people who have had a paranormal experience to remain quiet about it. Maybe that's the greatest achievement of the dead: they've convinced the world that they don't exist, so the majority of us are either disinterested in proving it otherwise or too convinced in our own beliefs to recognize a new viewpoint. Yet most of us are at least curious to know what happens when we die; some may say that information is even a right of humanity, that if another world exists after our physical bodies die, then it's our right to know about it.

I wrote this book for several reasons. First, I want to take you on my seven-year journey through the world of paranormal investigation from the documentary film in 2004 through the many seasons of *Ghost Adventures*. I want to tell you about the things that didn't make it onto the screen and dig deeper into the most significant events that did. We sometimes spend four days filming an episode and have to boil it down into one hour, so there's always stuff we want to show, but don't have the time to. And sometimes even the most significant phenomena that we capture have to be covered quickly because of time constraints.

Second, I want to use our adventures to address leading theories on life after death. Most paranormal investigators only seek to answer one singular question: Do ghosts exist? This approach is too narrowly focused and too shallow. I believe there needs to be a study on the bigger picture. I don't claim to be a quantum physicist, but I think some of the leading theories of quantum mechanics can help explain the paranormal in terms of natural physical occurrences. Quantum mechanics suggest the paranormal phenomena that we investigate is not only real, but also can be explained as natural processes of the universe. I think the two fields could mutually support each other, so I will take examples from my investigations and use them to explore the possible explanations.

Third, I want to instruct an interested individual on how to make contact with the other side by conducting a proper paranormal investigation. There are inherent risks and benefits of ghost hunting that need to be understood before buying a boatload of expensive equipment and staking out a cemetery at midnight. I'm not telling you to go out and hunt for ghosts, but if you're going to, then let me educate you on the process that will give you the best chance for success.

Finally, I want you to experience an investigation through my eyes. I want you to feel what it's like to be scared, pushed, cold, sluggish, whispered to, creeped out, and touched by an ethereal being or a demonic spirit. It's not like trying to pinpoint the cause of a knock in your bathroom in the middle of the night. The feeling is oppressive, heavy, sometimes evil, magnetic, and even addictive. I want you to know what your body goes through when the flight instinct tells you to run and the intense emotional struggle you can go through when you try to ignore it. When you're already amped up, physically and psychologically, simple noises seem much greater than they are. You don't just hear them—you feel the shockwave from them as well and have to train yourself to deal with them appropriately. It's a lifestyle that takes years to adjust to and I want to pass on those emotions and experiences.

Are You a Skeptic?

Before we go any further, I would like you to ask yourself this question. Are you going to read the rest of this book with an open mind? Many scientists and skeptics are quick to call researchers in the paranormal field shysters, cheats, and profiteers. While there certainly are those types out there, many of us are legitimately trying to perform research in the same manner as traditional scientists. We seek answers through a scientific process of observation, theory, hypothesis, experimentation, and analysis. Traditional scientists seek answers through the known laws of the universe, while people like me seek the same truths by understanding the unknown phenomena around us. We are very alike in our goals, but approach the question from different ends of the spectrum. While I don't pretend to represent the entire field of paranormal research, I want to be an advocate for its advancement, since the burden of proof has always been on our side of the question (which I don't necessarily agree with). I think it's unfortunate that skeptics and believers stand on different sides of the issue and point fingers at each other instead of working together to find answers. It's even more unfortunate that skeptics only scoff at believers instead of offering solutions. The skeptic community doesn't take the time to develop theories or take action to disprove the existence of spirits. They choose a passive approach of disbelief instead of scientific inquiry, which I would like to see change.

I've had many experiences with the afterlife and believe there are forces of nature that we simply do not yet understand. I know that ghosts exist. I know that spirits of the dead roam the physical world. I know that there's another realm beyond death that cannot be ignored, which is why I've dedicated my life to understanding it. The irony is that I was a skeptic myself until a paranormal experience changed my life irrevocably. I have now transformed into a sensitive; a person who is able to detect when spirits are present. It's a skill that's evolved over hundreds of paranormal investigations and has taught me that the human body is the best means of paranormal detection. I've become a fine-tuned instrument of spiritual sensitivity.

Although I've made believers out of many people, by no means do I want a following of sycophants and gullibles; in fact, I respect your right to question everything. There are those who will not believe in the afterlife, no matter what I provide as evidence in these pages or on TV. Those are two-dimensional mediums that cannot convey the senses of touch, taste, or smell and are limited in realistically capturing sights and sounds. That's why I like to take people on investigations personally to let them feel the forces at work there. Nothing can replace the feeling of actually being there when a spirit makes its presence known.

Many people are taught from an early age that the idea of spirits walking the Earth is impossible, and therefore won't even entertain the prospect of it, despite the evidence. You might be one of those people; if so, I only ask that you open your mind and realize that there are many forces on Earth that we simply don't yet understand. I'll be the first to admit that not all of those forces are paranormal, and could be perfectly explainable by physical and cognitive means. But before you go hiding behind the walls of scientific dogma, let's remember that science was once convinced that the world was flat and disbelievers were burned at the stake as heretics. Science is continually evolving, and the goal of paranormal investigators should be to augment scientific discovery to better understand the world around us. Scientific researchers readily admit that they only understand about 25 percent of the world around us, and only about 50 percent of the human brain. That leaves a lot to be discovered and explained, including the paranormal.

I'm not writing this book from the standpoint of someone who wants to convince you that the paranormal exists. Instead, I want to present the evidence for you and let you draw your own conclusions. Although I'm a believer in the afterlife, it's only through hard work and determined investigation that we as a people can endeavor to discover which side of the "do ghosts exist" question is correct. For that reason, I prefer to work with scientists rather than against them. Throughout this book, I will give the skeptics their time on the pulpit to promote their position. After all, that's only fair.

Here we go.

The thing that visited me as a child

SECTION

I

Beginnings

I think all adults tend to look back on their childhood and think they were a little strange. I'm not that naïve, so I'll break it down into more pragmatic terms—I had a paranormal experience at an early age. Many nights I would be visited by a large, dark creature that didn't look human. It rifled through my drawers and tossed my belongings around my room as I watched from under my covers. Still to this day I can draw an exact detailed sketch of what this animalistic apparition looked like.

It sounds silly and I never revealed it until I was an adult, but it happened. As a kid, I had no idea what the paranormal was and didn't care. All I knew was a supernatural intruder visited my room, so I remained scared and motionless out of self-preservation until it left. It could have been the product of an overactive mind, a true Elemental trying to force me to leave his house, or just a mischievous elf who needed underwear. It even left me items under my pillow like some maniacal tooth fairy. Truthfully, at the time, I didn't care what it was as long as it didn't harm me.

Little did I know that one day the paranormal would *become* my life. But how could I know? Few children know what they want to be when they grow up, and I was no different. I was born in Washington, D.C., and moved to Clearwater, Florida, as a young child of divorce with a pacifier in my mouth and still months away from taking my first steps. I was raised by my mother and stepfather as a typical Florida beach kid; crabbing, fishing, boating, and surfing. It was a normal family for the most part. I collected football and baseball cards, read comic books (my favorite was *Ghost Rider*, ironically), was obsessed with Dracula, and had a good relationship with my older sister. My mother was an interior designer and my stepfather worked in law enforcement as a deputy chief of police.

In high school I got my first car. An ugly, four-hundred-dollar, 1982, two-toned blue Ford Fairmont with home speaker cabinets in the back seats. I knew the car would never be taken seriously, so I converted it into a beach wagon by dumping sand on the floorboards. It seemed like the right thing to do because I spent so much time at the beach. I loved surfing, but with so many surfers becoming shark snacks each year, I had a natural affinity and healthy respect for the dangers of the ocean. The thing that scared me the most about the ocean was the feeling of being out in the open water, at the mercy of something uncontrollable.

Sitting on the beach was my release, my anchor that I could always turn to when things got bad. I loved the feel of the sand, the song of the waves, and the allure of the salt water. When thunderstorms rolled in, I would head out to Dunedin beach and watch the water go from light blue and recreational to a mean, dark, sinister attitude that reflected the weather. I don't

Oregon Coast.

know what it was, but watching something turn from docile to dangerous, and watching people leave while I held my ground, made me feel strong. But in addition to my anchor, these moments were also something more to me. Seeing the surface turn gray and creepy made me want to go out into the water even more than when it was blue and calming. As I'd leave the beach behind and venture out into the open water, I'd experience a whole new bag of emotions. Every time my toes touched the water, my nirvana instantly turned into my nightmare. While sitting in the murky water while everyone else ran from the beach was an adrenaline high and my moment of Zen, it also opened darkness in my mind. So you could say I've had a life-long love-hate relationship with the ocean. It's been my anchor, but not always in a good way.

A part of this dark feeling stemmed from a recurring dream. I've always had a vivid dream of being a deckhand on a Colonial-era ship crossing the ocean. The dream never changes. I'm never me, but rather someone else in eighteenth-century ruffled garb caught on the deck in a roaring nor'easter. Though I try to hold on, I always fall into the water and watch as the ship carries on without me. Alone and adrift I tread water as long as I can before the irresistible force of the ocean eventually drags me under and I wake in a fright.

Maybe the dream is a past-life memory. It wouldn't surprise me, because I've had other past-life messages. To this day, I'm convinced I was once a gold miner. I don't know how I feel about reincarnation, but for as long as I can remember, I have always felt a strong allure to the hearty nineteenth-century lifestyle of setting out on your own to strike it rich digging for gold. When we drove to North Carolina for family vacations, I couldn't pass a creek or cave without wanting to jump in and start panning. I had no idea why this urge was so strong as a kid, but I felt an incredible pull to creeks and mountains. They were places where I felt I belonged. Later in life I found myself walking through Virginia City, Nevada, getting flash images of me mining. I tasted the dust from the desert and knew I had been there before. I could see my coworkers, guys with beards. I could feel the vibrations of the pickaxes hitting the walls of the mines.

Is it just coincidence that my ghost adventures began in a mining town where we captured a full-bodied apparition?

Although I now have a deeper understanding of what my dreams and visions mean, as a child, I wasn't seeing any connection to what panning for gold and the ocean meant in my life. In high school I was still undecided on what I wanted to be. I was attracted to meteorology and broadcast journalism, but all I really knew was that I didn't want to be labeled. I was restless and grew easily tired of just about anything—classes, girls, places, hangouts—except my friends. They were always constant. I'd like to say I had attention deficit disorder, but I got good grades and knew how to focus myself when I needed to, so that's probably a lame excuse. I simply wasn't the type to let life pass me by, so adventure and conquest was always in the back of my mind. I didn't want to be Indiana Jones so much, but Batman? Absolutely.

In 1994 my mom and stepfather announced that we were moving to Lake Tahoe, California. It wasn't my first choice of places to live. I'd been visiting my dad in Chicago most years and had developed a good relationship with him and two kids up there, Phil and Sky, so instead of picking up stakes and moving to California, I left Florida in my senior year of high school and went to live with my dad in Chicago. Phil, Sky, and I became inseparable that year as we attended Glenbard West High School (the same place where the movie *Lucas* was filmed with

Charlie Sheen). I loved that school, but my stay there was short. Because of good grades I was allowed to graduate in January 1995 instead of with the rest of the class in June. I never got to wear a cap and gown, but it didn't matter to me. With the shackles of high school tossed aside, I was free to explore the world around me. So where did I go first? Detroit.

It's not exactly the windswept Sahara or the Amazonian Jungle, but it was the first step on the road to anything. My father had family in Grosse Ile, just outside the city. I wasn't there long (about eight months) when I decided to attend college at Western Michigan University.

Huge mistake.

Two weeks was all it took to realize college wasn't for me. It wasn't the academic work that made me so uncomfortable, but rather the overwhelming feeling that I was losing my identity. All around me I saw people whose goal in life was to commute to work, say hi to Sally the secretary, sit in a cubicle, and pretend to be happy for eight to ten hours a day just for the security of a fixed income. I guess you could say my mentality was like Peter from *Office Space* (although I would've loved to work with Milton and steal his red stapler). There was no risk, no edge-of-your-seat leap of faith into the unknown, no *joie de vivre*. It just wasn't me.

As you can imagine, dropping out of college was an instant sore spot with my father, especially after such a promising high school career. He couldn't understand my desire to do something that at least had the potential to be dangerous. I moved out, trying to find what I was looking for. I didn't.

Instead, I moved to Las Vegas, Nevada, with my mother and stepfather trying to find . . . something. I got a job as a mobile DJ MC'ing a lot of weddings, and although I didn't really care for the job, I recognized that it was an important day in many people's lives, so I took it seriously. Plus, I loved music too much to turn it down (though to this day I can't listen to "Celebration" without feeling nauseous). Music has always been a powerful influence in my life, and I have earbuds permanently embedded in my skull to prove it.

In Vegas I tried college again (this time Community). I did well, but found nothing but restlessness when I was accepted at UNLV. Reason told me I needed to get a degree and be a model citizen, but ambition always got the better of me.

Fun fact—In 1997 my sister and I were on Wheel of Fortune's Family Week. When Pat Sajak asked me what I did for a living, I panicked and said, "I teach everyone how to do the chicken dance."

I decided to move back to Detroit, and that's when things got dangerous. 1998–2002 were the roughest years of my life. I was trying to figure out who I was and I held lots of crappy jobs, including selling urinal screens and sanitary services, being a valet, party host, landscaper, and DJ again. I was just waiting for something to happen and until it did, I focused on physical challenges.

It was during this time that I got hooked on mixed martial arts. Some people know it as cage fighting or ultimate fighting, and many are quick to label it as brutality. To me it's the ultimate contest of skill waged by men who respect each other more than in any other sport. I traveled with my friend Dave Vitkay to many MMA tournaments, and I soon started training on my own. For the record, if I ever have to defend myself, I prefer to take a fight to the ground and pound my enemy out. It's a natural fit for me.

The other natural fit in my life was weight lifting. I was

always a skinny kid, but for my fifteenth birthday I got a set of push up bars and went crazy on them. I did a hundred push-ups a day and I suddenly started getting a chest. I started noticing that this skinny kid was getting stronger and was building confidence. Even my friends in Detroit noticed my physical gains. I weighed 175 pounds but could lift more than my 225-pound friends. Physical strength fueled me. All my life I had been suffering from panic and anxiety disorder, and my physical activity helped me battle them.

But despite these releases in my life, things were still going downhill. My friends weren't problem starters, but we always seemed to end up in trouble and fights. I've never started a fight in my life, and in fact I don't like violence, but trouble always seemed to find us. It wore me down, and my train was completely off the tracks and ready to plummet over the cliff. For over a year I'd been working at an AT&T Wireless store selling cell phones (I still can't believe I stuck out a retail job that long) and just wasn't happy. I couldn't find myself and it was the darkest point in my life.

Suddenly, my mother enrolled me in the Motion Picture Institute of Michigan. Mom understood me. She could see that I needed something more. I fell in love with the art of documentary filmmaking and graduated with honors in an elite class. I went completely overboard with my final project, which was supposed to be a two-minute film that I turned into a full-length movie with a twenty-page script and local actors. It was called *The Red Butterfly*.

That was the first event that started pulling me out of the abyss I was staring down, but I was still unhappy. I started praying to a higher power. I knew that I had a very unique, specific purpose in my life and I asked Him what it was. God responded by slapping me.

In my wildest dreams I never imagined I could have an encounter with a ghost. It was the last thing I expected as an answer to my prayers. I was living in an apartment building on the edge of Elizabeth Park in the historic, gentrified district of Trenton, Michigan. In my apartment I could feel the presence of something that was not inviting, but I actually liked it. It was like being in the gray, murky water of Florida again by myself when most people ran for cover.

Seven nights in a row during the summer of 2002, a female ghost would scream my name, Zachary, at the top of her lungs. At first I thought it was a dream, but then I realized it was happening and I could not control it. On the seventh night she upped the ante to get her point across. I was lying in bed, face down, when she screamed my name and then pressed down on me so hard that I couldn't get up. I was pinned to my bed, unable to move, and started panicking. As strong as I was I couldn't escape the weight she brought to bear on my back. When she finally let me up, I turned over and saw her looking at me. There was eye contact and I felt a shockwave of energy from her. I stared at her, unable to look away. This spirit wanted me to see her and to this day I have not looked at an apparition that looked into me like this. I stumbled outside and tried to rationalize what had happened, certain I was going to die from a heart attack. It was an unmistakable moment that created a new dimension in my mind and opened it up to the paranormal.

When there's a common threat, people become one and find a purpose together. I finally felt like I had a purpose in life. I was so close to joining the other side, but instead those on the other side created a path for me to avoid going over the cliff. That path led me to Las Vegas, which led me to where I am today.

I want to be clear that I was indifferent on the topic of ghosts at the time. But every night this harbinger was there, taunting me, daring me, challenging me, because that's the way I saw it. Everyone responds to a paranormal experience differently. Some run from it. Some embrace it. I was traumatized and frightened, but also incredibly motivated to understand what had happened.

I had a thousand questions, mostly of a physical nature. How could an ethereal being have physical properties? How could a dead person make sound and create force? Does she sleep? Is she bored? Is she mischievous? Does she know she's dead? How did she know my name? Does she know the air-speed velocity of an unladen swallow? I wanted to know if life is just rock, soil, air, water, and fire—or if there is more. Are there spiritual aspects that people ignore?

But it wasn't the time for answers yet. I couldn't stay in Trenton and wrote "this place is haunted" with a permanent black marker on the back of a cabinet just before heading back to Las Vegas. Detroit is a rough town, and though I love it, I'm happy to be alive after some of the things that happened during that period. That book is closed, locked, and sent to the bottom of the sea never to be reopened again, but those times made me strong and banished my fears of the physical world. From the adversity of those years I came out feeling invincible and hungry for success.

But the voice of that spirit was ever present, a calling that made no sound, yet I heard it clearly. She kept telling me to find answers and I was convinced that I finally had meaning in my life. I felt I was chosen to immerse myself in the unknown and unlock the mysteries of our world.

Destiny? Is That You?

I met Nick Goff during a wedding and found him to be an instant kindred spirit. Like me, he attended film school and had a paranormal experience years earlier. By mid-2003 we were partners making high-end wedding videos, commercials, and video projects for Vegas acts like Penn and Teller, Siegfried and Roy, and Rita Rudner. Then one day he told me about his experience on a ghost hunting trip in Virginia City and the mining towns around it.

Click.

It was all clear to me. At that very moment I saw a way to combine my curiosity in the afterlife with my passion for filmmaking. Nick and I decided we would set out on a mission to document an apparition on film in the historic haunted mining towns of the area. But we knew two cameras weren't enough. We needed a third, and it had to be cheap; someone willing to work for nothing, since that's all we had. Nick threw out Aaron Goodwin's name and we met him one night at The Road Runner in Las Vegas. It felt right. The three of us had good chemistry and we decided to go for it. But there was an obvious problem. We weren't paranormal investigators. We were simply three curious guys armed with cameras and in our youthful exuberance, thought that was actually a good thing.

A road trip through Nevada's desolate mining country might not sound like fun, but I reveled in the moment. We drove to remote towns like Goldfield, Gold Hill, and Rhyolite, which turned out to be scarier than the filming. We started in the windswept town of Tonopah, where coyotes outnumber people. Our first paranormal investigation (which it could only loosely be called) was an old hotel called The Castle House. I swear the original owner invented the telegraph it was so old.

The current owners clearly thought we were nuts when we unloaded bags of equipment and a Ouija board during the worst thunderstorm I'd ever seen. The lightning was so intense that I swore I was going to get struck and killed carrying a tripod. Not my preferred way to die. Inside the hotel was a macabre scene of playful horror. Over a hundred dolls were strewn about an upstairs room staring at us like a jury of weird. Things happened that evening that didn't make it into the documentary. Doors opened and closed on their own as if someone was using them, aromas of perfume wafted through the air like scarlet women, and of course there was static electricity—enough to power Las Vegas for millennia it seemed.

In Virginia City our quest morphed from fun adventure to deadly serious mission. The people of the desert were affectless, like walking puppets of the dead. We chalked their demeanors up to having daily ghostly experiences and left it at that. Being in Virginia City was like going back in time. I was told a prostitute had killed herself in the bathtub of our room at the Silver Queen Hotel, so to tempt fate I slept in it. Several times I heard water splashing around me from what we thought was a lady spirit who didn't like people in her room. In the middle of the night, Nick and I heard knocking on the room's door and saw a mist coming through it at the same time. We captured it on film and knew right then that our lives were about to change.

But it was another event that changed our lives forever. At the Goldfield Hotel in Goldfield, Nevada, we felt a heavy force bidding us to leave. It was hard to move, like walking through a pool with ankle weights. Nick wasn't himself. He was lethargic and moved in and out of coherence. In the basement of the hotel, we knew something otherworldly was present with us. Discarded bricks in a dark corner drew us in when suddenly one flew across the room in an arc that scared the living crap out of us. It was almost painful when it happened because it honestly felt like arrows shooting through our skin. The message was clear—"Get out of here!"

We complied.

I still wonder what would have happened if we had stayed. That event is one of the reasons I wanted to do this full-time and return to get answers someday (we would have two more incidents with this hotel in the following years—more on that later).

We captured voices on our digital recorders that we didn't hear until long after we returned to Las Vegas. That was one of our first lessons of paranormal investigation: disembodied voices usually occur at a frequency lower than normal human ears can detect, so you don't even know that you've captured a spirit voice until you rewind the recorder and listen (recorders can pick up sounds above and below normal hearing range).

After a year of putting the material together, we submitted the finished product, titled *Ghost Adventures*, to the New York International Film and Video Festival and won their prize for best documentary film. It was also nominated for best feature film at the Eerie Horror Film Festival in 2006. Finally, NBC Universal picked it up to air seven times in a year on the Syfy Channel where it made their top ten list. The snowball started rolling.

We formed the Ghost Adventures Crew network, a group of like-minded paranormal investigators across the country. Suddenly I was being recognized in public and found myself talking to fans for hours. Usually I'm the one wanting to talk to people about my experiences, but after the film aired people approached me about the film and their experiences. It was a weird role reversal that took a lot of getting used to and I'm still not completely at ease with it. I always considered myself an average guy who experienced something extraordinary and wanted to share it with the world, not a celebrity.

I met a man named Wayne Allen Root who was experienced in television, and I asked him if he would help me turn the documentary into a television show. He pointed me in the right direction and introduced me to the right people. During those pitch meetings I would get emotional and physically shake at the opportunity to bring the paranormal to the world, but to be honest, I was shaking for another reason. I still suffered from social anxiety disorder and had a hard time speaking in front of a group of people. Before my paranormal experience, I would stutter, stammer, sweat, and become generally scared at the thought of being the center of attention. After coming face to face with a ghost, those feelings slowly subsided. During the making of the documentary I discovered that what most people call creepy, scary, and spooky, I call comfy, cozy, and home.

Two weeks after pitching the idea to the Travel Channel they offered us a full season of *Ghost Adventures*. Our charisma and chemistry made us likable enough and our investigation style gave us credibility. It was gratifying because it verified that we did the documentary right, despite having no experience in the field. We showed that we could advance the paranormal science and that a lot of people believed in us.

I've been criticized over the years for sensationalizing our investigations and overreacting to the evidence we collect. I don't deny that I get excited, but that's what happens when you're passionate about what you do. I am a paranormal investigator to the core. Every part of me is invested in this life and is completely committed to finding paranormal entities and bringing them to light. Would you want it any other way?

Fast Facts about Zak

I get some of the weirdest questions, so I'd like to dispel a few myths and throw out some fast facts about me:

- I've never worshipped the devil, studied the secrets of voodoo, or drunk blood for protection from evil spirits.
- I've never been called a savior or a patron saint.
- I've never battled a zombie, Ninja'd a ghoul, or rode a bull.
- I've never been referred to as "The Zak."
- I like science fiction, think baseball is boring, and believe artificial sweetener is worth the extra calories.
- I'm a great wingman.
- I think Star Wars is better than Star Trek.
- I fantasize about having a beer with Chevy Chase.
- I have one scar underneath each eyebrow from falling into a glass table as a kid and from a particularly nasty hammock incident.
- I have five tattoos.
- I've had a stalker and had to issue a restraining order against him.
- I now have a concealed weapons permit.
- I'm addicted to history because today's fast-paced, technological society wears me down and the rugged, simpler life of years gone by is enticing.
- I'm very much a believer in Karma and what goes around comes around.
- My biggest influences are the deceased people I meet. Growing up it was Ralph Waldo Emerson.
- Wounded veterans choke me up.
- Animal cruelty is the shame of mankind.

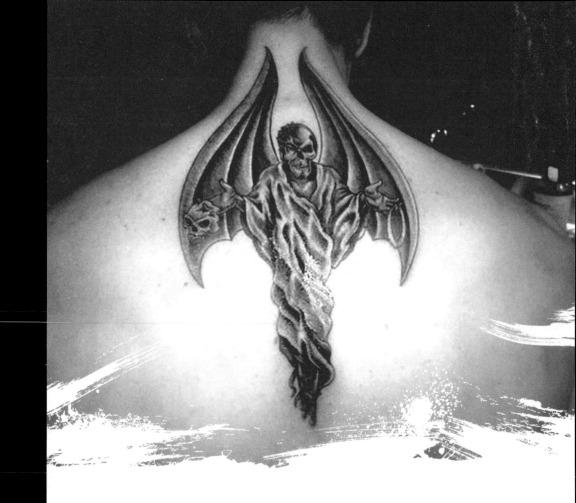

Back tattoo—

Symbolizes my experience in Poveglia, Italy.

Fight between good and evil.

SECTION

Innocence

hosts get a bad rap. If we believed everything that came out of Hollywood, then ghosts would throw hatchets, push people over cliffs, and possess entire kitchens that just happen to be full of sharp knives. After several years of doing this job, I can verify the exact opposite is true. Sure there are demons and wraiths who seek to harm the living, but there are just as many virtuous, misunderstood spirits with good intentions as there are mischievous and evil ones. Crossing over from the physical realm to the spiritual side does not instantly make someone a bad person (and let's remember these are still people in a nonphysical form). There are spirits whose desire to help people carries over with them. There are confused spirits who just want answers, and there are child spirits who just want to play.

Energy

Before we set a single foot in the afterlife, it's critical to understand the one core assumption that just about every paranormal theory hinges on: **spirits are composed of weak energy and are not capable of manifesting themselves into sound or sight until they come in contact with a greater amount of energy that they can borrow or take altogether**. The presence of an energy source gives them the ability to manifest as sight or sound. This is key to understanding the paranormal. I believe in this theory and in fact it's probably the one constant I've found throughout my travels and observations with the paranormal. Spirits can gather energy from just about anything: electronic equipment, lights, cameras, batteries, cars, EMF pumps, water, and even human beings. One of the reasons I believe the Rolling Hills Asylum is such a hotbed of paranormal activity is because it sits directly across the street from a power generation plant, giving the spirits inside something to feed off of. It's the one core theory that has pervaded this field and proven to be true over the decades of recorded paranormal science.

Supporting this theory is the Law of Energy Conservation, which states that energy can neither be created nor destroyed in a closed system. According to this law, all energy in the universe has already been made and our physical bodies are merely containers for our own personal energy. If the body is a container of energy, then when it dies its energy is released back into the universe the same way air is released back into the atmosphere when a balloon pops.

But does it remain intact with all of its knowledge, experiences, emotions, and identity or does it simply dissipate back into the environment and lose everything that it was? This is a critical question for our field and one of the keys we all seek to unlock. The prevailing theory in the paranormal community is that a person's energy remains intact and either moves to a new plane (heaven or hell) or resides in the physical plane with us, which causes what we call a haunting. It is this wandering energy that still knows who it is with which we try to make contact.

When spirits manifest there is almost always a physical change in the world around me. It could be as simple as a flickering light or as severe as a complete drain on my equipment, but in almost every piece of evidence I've ever captured, it's there: an unmistakable transfer of energy from a known source to an unknown receiver.

The source can even be us. Humans store energy. It's a fact. And because no sighting of a spirit can happen without a human observer present, it's assumed that ghosts borrow the energy of the living to build strength and make their presence known through sight or sound. It's why people sometimes feel suddenly lethargic or the hairs on their arms and neck stand up. It's a physical response to their personal energy being gathered by ghosts and almost always precedes a paranormal encounter.

I have felt spirits use my own life energy many times. At first it was scary (naturally), but now I love it because I know I'm making a connection. I can feel the shockwaves of them using me and I become a part of the experience. I become the battery that helps them connect to the physical world. The paranormal experience goes up a level from two-dimensional to three, which makes it that much more real and intense.

There's no question, spirits will draw energy from anything they can get their hands on. How can you argue with what happened at Ohio State Reformatory when we were walking around and had five different pieces of electronic equipment fail and be drained of their power at the same time that we felt physical changes and paranormal activity kicked up.

Higher emotion equals higher energy. When you become angry you sweat, you stammer your words, and your skin gets hot. Now imagine the vortex of emotions when there's a murder, rape, or traumatic death. All those emotions now become supercharged. It's like running the RPMs in a race car into the red zone. It doesn't have to be the last emotions before death either. The extreme loneliness and depression of a broken heart can put your emotions in the red zone also. An inmate at Ohio State Reformatory set himself on fire in his cell. That was a supercharged emotional event like no other. I believe that the atmosphere becomes imprinted with that severe energy and it becomes ripe for residual hauntings. That's why you hear screams in haunted places from the supercharged emotional state.

It's important to understand this principle because most paranormal investigations rely on it—in order to manifest itself into sight or sound, a spirit has to pull together all its dissipated energy to make a human form and/or language and many times has to borrow energy from another source to complete the process. On numerous occasions I've had freshly charged batteries suddenly die and audio equipment fail unexpectedly just before I captured a piece of paranormal video or audio evidence. This is why using a single video camera is not a good idea, because the spirit could drain your only source of data gathering. It's also why having fresh batteries on hand is a must in paranormal investigation.

Schools, Reformatories, and Children

For most of us it's second nature to reach out to those less fortunate than ourselves or the victims of bad circumstances, especially when those victims are children. For millennia, virtuous people with deep pockets and influential connections have built institutions to care for the poor, the destitute, and the abandoned. Hundreds of schools and reformatories have been built to care for the youth of the world, almost always with the best intentions, but rarely immune to bad tidings.

One of the saddest aspects about these types of institutions is that children were frequently dropped off and abandoned by families who could not care for them. Especially during the Great Depression and decades after, families who could not afford to care for their own kids would simply leave them on the doorsteps of the local reformatory to live a life with others who were placed there by the state for their crimes. So you had a situation where violent youths lived alongside abandoned kids who did nothing wrong, other than being born into a family that couldn't care for them. That's a recipe for suffering.

Schools and reformatories seem to pop up on everyone's list of most haunted places, but to be honest, I have a hard time believing that the spirits of children are left behind after death. Kids don't have the ability to decide whether they go to heaven or hell. They don't understand what those places are until around ten years old and even then they're just told that heaven is good and hell is bad. It's hard to wrap my head around the idea that spirits of children are still roaming the Earth, because what's more innocent than a child? What unfinished business would a child have that would keep its soul trapped here?

At the Villisca Axe Murder House, where several children

are known to have died, I couldn't find any evidence to support a child haunting. I might be convinced to believe in the child spirit who still looks for her mother at the Trans Allegheny Lunatic Asylum because there is some documented evidence that suggests she actually lived and died there and did not know who her mother was. But then again, I tried very hard to make contact with this child and was unsuccessful. I didn't have any luck finding a spirit of a child in the basement of the Houghton Mansion either.

Many believe the spirit of a small child was already residing in that basement when the Houghton's built their property on top of it. Several encounters down there with a mischievous ghost have been reported, from voices to giggling to shirt tugging. There's even a story of a ball that moved on its own after being set in the middle of the basement.

I sat in the frozen, still basement trying to make contact. Usually there's some sort of ambient noise during an investigation or even a wisp of air, but this cellar was absolutely still. Not even my rickety metal chair squeaked. I placed a small plastic ball in the middle of the room and asked a few leading questions, hoping it would move or that I'd capture a giggle or shirt tug. Instead I got the sound of a pair of old coke bottles being clanged together, like something out of the end of the movie *The Warriors*. This place was deathly quiet, so the noise was loud enough that it startled me.

I jumped out of my chair and ran toward the ball, but it hadn't moved. It was exactly where I left it, as still as could be. I looked around for anything that could have caused the noise, but found nothing. There was no glass, no metal, no manmade objects that could have been the source of the noise. I was mystified, and to this day, I have no idea who or what was down there with me, but I don't think it was the spirit of a kid.

Child hauntings are challenging because they can be a couple of different things. They can either be haunting in the traditional sense or a demon trying to use the sounds of children to confuse us. When you hear about a child haunting, it almost always involves laughter, which evil entities are very good at mocking. I think it's possible that darker, bullying spirits uses child spirits like bait. But it is also possible that there could be a building with a demon and no child spirits at all. I've investigated buildings that echoed of laughter, but had no reported history of kids living or dying in them, which leads me to believe that there aren't really kids in there.

Trigger Objects

If someone stole my iPod, I would probably be enraged. It's something that I use every day and an object that I covet because I am so influenced by music. That's the philosophy behind trigger objects. The ball at the Houghton Mansion was an inanimate trigger object. It's a simple tool that can be used to elicit paranormal activity through the emotional attachment that the spirit had to the object. It can be anything the spirit once owned or just admired—a vase, a picture, an old football trophy—anything it felt a connection to while it was alive. It's like putting a treat on the floor for a mouse and hoping he comes out of his hole to investigate it.

Like I said, my iPod is my personal trigger object. I live through my music and use my iPod every day, so I think if I were roaming the Earth as a dispossessed soul and saw someone holding it, I would have an emotional reaction and my spirit would make a noise or even manifest as a mist or apparition. That's the goal behind using them.

39

Probably my most successful trigger object was a teddy bear that we used in the Edinburgh Vaults in Scotland. The Vaults are the definition of creepy. Dark, damp, smelly, and musty, they have seen some of the worst humanity has to offer after centuries of the poor and violent living in their bowels. Death was common in the Vaults, and it was one of the most active paranormal places I've ever been (and one of my favorites, but that's a different story).

Many people have seen or heard the spirit of a child in the Vaults, so during our investigation there, I took a teddy bear to the room where the spirit's voice has been heard often and left it there. I set up a static night vision camera along with an EMF detector and left the room to investigate a different chamber. Minutes later the video camera captured the teddy bear moving with no one in the room. The teddy bear didn't just move a little, it moved a lot, far too much to be caused by wind or a simple imbalance. It also turned in two ways on two different axes. First it spun slightly to the right and then it tilted backward as if acted on by an outside force on two different sides. Could it have been the spirit of a child trying to pick it up to play with it?

Besides the object's movement, there were other pieces of evidence to bolster the belief that this was paranormal. At the exact same moment that it moved, a high-pitched voice was captured in the room on the camera's audio and the EMF detector spiked. So one electronic device and a meter captured evidence at the same time. It was one of the best moments of paranormal evidence captured on three different electronic devices at the same time. Those are the moments paranormal investigators live for, and it happened because of a trigger object.

Was it a child? I don't know. I can't say whether it was a kid trying to pick up a toy or an adult trying to kick it away. Maybe I don't want to accept that kids could be spirits because the thought of a deceased child reaching out to play with a toy stirs a personal sadness in me. That's one kid who never got a chance to be a kid. He never grew to experience life, to feel the uncertainty of casting himself out into the world, the immense joy of a first date, and the comfort of close friends being there when things go bad. Accepting this notion also means they've experienced the pain of death, which I have a hard time stomaching. That sadness can be just as life altering as the violent demons that have attacked me.

Another form of trigger object (and one that is more effective) is the human being. It stands to reason that if a ghost has an emotional attachment to an object and can be goaded into manifesting when it sees or hears that object, then contact with a person it knew or cared for in life will cause the same reaction. The presence of a human can be just as effective as an inanimate object and sometimes even more so. Imagine you have died and find yourself unable to leave the house you lived in for ten years. Suddenly, you see your now grown-up daughter walking past the exact spot where you died. You would have a severe emotional reaction and would probably gather enough energy to be seen or heard. That's the goal of using humans as trigger objects.

Of course the drawback is the risk to the person involved. In the scenario above, a woman who feels the presence of her deceased dad could fall into emotional trauma of her own, which is the last thing I want. They could also be attacked by the spirit with whom you're trying to make contact if it's not who or what you thought it was.

While investigating the Villisca Axe Murder House in Iowa, I spent time with some people who had lived there when they were young and who had seen firsthand the apparitions of the children who were murdered within its walls. Just being back in the house shook them to their core and it was clear that the emotional state of those former residents was too fragile to use them as human trigger objects, so I never even considered it.

Some spirits have a connection to all people in general instead of one particular person. I've encountered spirits who like to grope women and others who like to be in the company of men. For these ghosts, it's not one specific person like a mother or brother that causes them to manifest, but any person who ventures into their sphere. These types of spirits are a little easier to bring out into the open because they show a desire to make contact.

One of my more infamous encounters with a human trigger object was during an investigation at the Ohio State Reformatory in Mansfield, Ohio. We took a woman named Sarah who volunteered at the prison and sent her alone into one of the darkest cellblocks of the building where many tales of men being attacked and females being groped had been reported. My reasoning was simple—the one thing men miss the most while incarcerated are women, so it made sense that the former inmates would react to her. Every time I use a female as a trigger object in a place like this, I get a response, and with so many stories of women having personal experiences in this prison, it made sense that a lonely female would incite a response. I was right.

Before she even left our side, Sarah felt breathing on the back of her neck and captured two EVPs with a digital recorder in her hands. One was of heavy breathing while the other one said, "Run Sarah." Looking back on it, I believe this was a warning from a responsible spirit who knew what would happen to her if she stayed too long in the prison alone.

Digital recorders and the Electronic Voice Phenomena (EVP) that they capture are the backbones of paranormal investigation. EVPs are recordings of disembodied voices that are captured at a lower frequency than normal human hearing can detect, and they are a crucial element for determining whether or not spirits are present. EVPs have been used since the 1920s, but have evolved a great deal as the technology has improved.

Sarah then walked through the cellblock without us. I commended her for her courage and willingness to help our cause, but I was also a little concerned for her safety. Sarah was like a tasty minnow blindly swimming through a pool of sharks. Sooner or later one (or more) of them would bite.

"Was that you that brushed the back of my hair?" she asked strolling by herself down the rows of rusty and worn cells while I waited with Nick and Aaron about thirty feet away.

"Sorry, Sarah. Sorry," came a disembodied response that we discovered on her digital recorder later. Minutes after that, as Aaron was experiencing his own paranormal activity, we heard Sarah yelling for help. "Could someone please come down here?" her voice echoed off the walls with the distinct ring of suppressed fear. We ran to her.

"Something pulled my hair," she said, doing a good job of containing her emotions. She was brave, but I could also tell something had just happened that rattled her. As she walked down the corridor, an unseen hand grabbed her hair and pulled it backward, causing her head to snap back. Her presence had the exact effect I was hoping for—a spirit, probably a male inmate unaccustomed to being around women, attacked her. Rather than run, Sarah stood her ground and called out to us, though we were slow to respond because we were also experiencing our own paranormal encounters at the same time.

Trigger objects like Sarah are very effective at enticing paranormal activity, but they're also important for gauging the mental capacity of the spirits involved. A disembodied voice apologizing to Sarah shows responsibility, accountability, and even remorse. It says the spirit didn't want to hurt her, but wanted to make contact and wasn't sure how. It also made it clear that there was more than one spirit in that cellblock—one that wanted to hurt people and one that didn't.

An alternate explanation is that there was one spirit who both harmed her and then apologized for it. Either way, the activity and captured voices give us some insight as to what the spirits are thinking. That kind of evidence not only helps the singular investigation, but also the overall cause of paranormal investigators—to help the living communicate with the dead, which is enhanced through human trigger objects.

Good Spirits

The biggest challenge when communicating and interacting with spirits is that you start off the relationship like a blind man. The people you want to know more about are a complete mystery and their intentions are not clear, so there's a feeling-out process. Who am I really in company with? Should I go in with my guard up or arms open? Is this a genuine spirit or one who wants to do me harm? Is it going to be truthful with me or lie? Does it know it's dead?

Some people think it's easy to make contact, but that's only the first step. Understanding a ghost is a completely different thing. Sometimes it's like reaching out to a cute fuzzy bunny that suddenly grows fangs and attacks you like the rabbit in *Monty Python and the Holy Grail*. The paranormal world is so camouflaged and dark. You can be lured or tricked by demonic entities, so your intuition is very important.

Even when you know the history of a building, it can be used against you. Halles-Bar Marina in Tennessee has a grave-yard full of children on the property, but the spirits inside are anything but innocent. This is a place where a combat veteran was more scared than anything he saw overseas. It's a place where I thought I was going to comfort children, but instead got attacked. So I always have my guard up. Fortunately, I don't always need it.

I specialize in confronting evil, dark entities like the ones at Ohio State Reformatory, but there are plenty of ghosts who don't mean any harm and just want to know what happened to them. There are spirits who can't rest because they want to find closure for how they died or have unfinished business. Many times they're just reaching out to communicate, which I am al-ways willing to do. That's one of the core principles of para-normal investigation—you have to be open-minded and walk into every situation without preconceived notions. Just because someone told you an evil spirit lurks in the basement of an abandoned warehouse does not mean you should be automati-cally confrontational during an investigation. You might also encounter a situation of multiple spirits with different agendas. You could be on one floor of a large building and encounter a spirit who wants to hurt or scare you, but on the next floor you encounter one who needs your help. Preston Castle in Ione, California, held just such a scenario.

Halfway between Sacramento and Stockton, Preston Castle was built in 1890 as a reformatory for young males, but long before that, its grounds had been used as a cemetery. During its time as a reformatory, Preston was witness to at least twelve deaths, including a boy who was shot in the back while trying to escape. The compound is massive and decorated in a gothic style that, along with its imposing bell tower, oozes mystery and an allure to discover its secrets.

When you look at Preston Castle, you just know it's haunted. It's like looking into a psychic's crystal ball, but not one from Spencer's gifts. It's the real deal. You can see the history there. You can see the juveniles that were sent there for their crimes. You can see the murders, the darkness, the lives that were wasted, and why it was shoved out into the middle of nowhere away from prying eyes.

But what you can't see is the mysterious murder of Anna Corbin. Anna was the head housekeeper who was found dead in 1957 in a basement closet. She had been dragged from the kitchen to the basement, bludgeoned beyond recognition and strangled. It was a horrible death for someone who certainly did not deserve it. An inmate was tried three times for the crime, but was never convicted for various reasons.

Before the investigation, a local reporter asked me to bring back any evidence I gathered about Anna's death, which took the night to a whole new level. This was no longer just a paranormal investigation, but a homicide investigation as well. I took that very seriously, but at the same time tried not to let it affect the way we do things. I was flattered that this man wanted us to help him solve a fifty-year-old crime, but we also had a job to do.

I brought a bouquet of flowers into the dusty basement and set them at the place where Anna's body was found. But as soon as I backed away from that spot, something happened that I've never talked about. I had an immediate and powerful emotional connection to the place where she died. The room looked different. My ears rang. I could smell something being cooked in the kitchen down the hall and I saw flash images of her life. I don't claim to be psychic, but in that moment I felt like I was there when Preston Castle and Anna Corbin were both alive and well. It was a surreal moment and I had to physically shake my head to tear away from what I was seeing, hearing, and feeling. It's hard to put into words, but if I had to, I'd simply say I was there . . . in the busy heyday of Preston Castle. It was like I time traveled and was fortunate enough to see how life was back then.

I kept that experience to myself until now. At first, reason told me to reject it . . . that it was not possible . . . that my senses were playing tricks on me, but I swear I was there in the moment and it was powerful. I think this is when I truly developed a sixth sense to feel their world. I felt like I was rewarded by a higher power for working so hard to communicate with the dead and ease their suffering.

This was one of the first times I realized I was more than a paranormal investigator. I had become a "sensitive"—someone who is in tune with the spirits of the deceased. It was the moment when things went deeper and I realized there was some kind of higher power that seemed to be graduating me from Mister Miyagi's basic school of "wax on, wax off" teaching and moving me onto a higher learning platform. The calling I once heard, which told me that this was my destiny, was suddenly verified. This was the golden moment where I was in the presence of a genuinely good spirit.

Suddenly, I felt two arms slide underneath mine, pick me up, and guide me away from the room. I don't remember the walking part at all and even after watching the video later, I don't remember it. I only remember moving through this giant, dark place with nothing to light my way like I knew exactly where I was and where I needed to be. Nick and Aaron called to me and asked where I was going, but their words echoed off the empty walls and I didn't respond. I even left my camera sitting on the floor, which I never do.

I walked through the castle to Anna's apartment on the third floor and sat in the middle of it, feeling a blanket of reassurance cover me like I never had before. I felt at peace in her room and really didn't want to leave. I felt like an old friend was watching me, and the room was full of teddy bears, ice cream, and Kenny G. I sat there as long as Nick and Aaron would let me, comfortable in the safety of her presence.

I think this was Anna's way of communicating. She didn't have enough energy to be heard or seen, so her way of communicating was to transfer her emotions onto me. I think she was a good person and wanted me to feel welcome instead of scared and did that by feeling at peace herself.

The common term for this interaction is emotional transference. It's the sudden feeling of a certain emotion that the observer was previously not feeling and which comes from an outside source. In the paranormal world, it's believed that a spirit can transfer its emotions onto a living person as it passes through or by them. If a spirit is angry, the observer suddenly is filled with rage, as happened to me a few times. If the spirit is sad, the observer will be, too. If you learn to identify this type of interaction, you can use it to help detect when spirits are present, especially if you have an EMF detector handy that can verify a jump in electromagnetic fields at the same time your emotions change.

Ghosts Changed My Life

I felt different after leaving Preston Castle. There was a shock factor to that investigation that I've only experienced a few times. It was like having a near-death experience and not looking at the world in the same light afterward. I was affected by the experience with Anna, but in a good way. Ghosts like this one empower me. It isn't well known, but I once had a severe social phobia. I couldn't be around people. I couldn't eat, write, or speak well with people. But after emotional events like this with spirits, I feel cured. I look at the world differently because I know something that most people either don't or won't accept. Moments like this at Preston Castle have made me stronger and I wish the same were true for others. Too many people look at paranormal encounters negatively. They're scared by the unknown and perceive a meeting with a ghost as frightening or evil when the opposite could be the real truth. Many times a spirit wants the help of the living or is trying to offer a human assistance, as it was for me with the spirit of Anna Corbin.

Another interesting thing happened in Anna Corbin's room that I didn't know about until after the investigation when I reviewed the video footage. A ball of light that had a very intelligent flight path clearly shot into my head while I sat in the middle of her room. This was not my first experience with this. At the Goldfield Hotel, a ball of light slowly followed the contour of my forearm at the same time that the temperature dropped and my skin became very cold. These were my first experiences with orbs, and I could not deny that they were connected to an increase in paranormal activity. Is it just coincidence that these balls of light (that are clearly not bugs or dust) are accompanied by emotional changes in myself and happen at the same time paranormal evidence is captured? The connection cannot be ignored.

Orbs

I do agree that approximately 95 percent of what people speculate to be "paranormal orbs" captured on still cameras and infrared camcorders can be debunked as environmental conditions and photographic error. However, I also strongly believe that the remaining 5 percent really are orbs of energy, partial manifestations of spirits, or visual and residual hauntings.

Many times light can bounce back directly into the lens of a camera and cause a perfectly round ball of whiteness on the exposure. Even more common are dust, moisture, pollen, snow, rain, cigarette ash, or a microscopic particle that gets in front of the lens and causes a reflection. We've all seen it happen. Video is different, though. The orbs I've captured on video move in random and intelligent directions and disappear into our bodies at the same time that physical changes occur. The consistent presence of orbs during other paranormal activity has led me to believe that they are indeed spirits, at least as far as video is concerned (I still think many orbs from digital and film cameras are easily debunked).

Unexplained lights are common during paranormal investigations. Many times I've seen flashes of light at the end of a hallway or in another room and was too slow to catch it on film. As I stated before, spirits are composed of energy. Energy frequently gives off light or transforms into light, so by the substitutive property (if a = b, and b = c, then a = c), it's easy to see how spirits can manifest as light. Knowing this, we have to ask the question, "What shape would that light take?"

When you think about it, the sphere is the perfect shape of the universe. A sphere represents equal pressure being exerted in all directions and is the primary shape of the cosmos. A bubble is a good example. A soap bubble floating through air forms a perfectly round shape (except for those huge wobbly bubbles you see courtyard entertainers make with their overly wet ropes that create a mess on the concrete where severe pedestrian accidents can occur by slipping . . . damn, am I rambling again?).

Anyway . . . the air inside the container is pushing outward with an equal and uniform amount of pressure in all directions, causing the bubble to take the shape of a round sphere or orb. If spirits are pure energy, then it stands to reason that they could also take the shape of a sphere with a thin layer containing them.

When I capture an orb on film, I go through all the possibilities to debunk it. As a young investigator, I would put the video through an oscilloscope to ensure it was not tampered with by an outside source or damaged en route from the investigation site to the studio. But as I became more experienced, I got to the point that I could visually discern an orb from an insect or dust by its physical characteristics. The composition and behavior of the object in question always gives it away.

Dust is fine and appears like snow on film, while bugs look more like rods with pulsating wings as they move into and out of frame. The movement of orbs is different. They have intelligent flight patterns. They go back and forth, side to side, and interact with humans, even hesitating before crashing into us. They have very discernable, identifiable patterns of behavior— and that's what always interests me.

Besides the physical debunking and elimination of all other variables in the equation, the one element that always makes me sure that an orb is paranormal is how it acts around the living and the effect it has on the people around it. The orbs always seem to behave like a person would and they appear at the same time we feel things happen to us or around us. Orbs frequently coincide with a physical reaction in me or someone in the investigation crew. Headaches, nausea, pain, and even the first stages of possession have happened in the presence of orbs. At Essex County Hospital we captured an orb as it flew into Nick's face. Seconds later, his skin was red and hot to the touch as if he'd been slapped. It's this behavior and correlation to other physical feelings that gives us telltale signs of a paranormal orb versus something else.

Anna Corbin's room is a good example. The orb we captured there shot into my head at the same time that I felt an undeniable wave of peace come over me. Again, I can't argue with the fact that this orb happened at the same time as a physiological change overtook me. It was some type of undeniable form of energy lacking the characteristics of natural entities like bugs or dust. I'm actually glad we captured this orb instead of a full apparition at this moment. It helps verify all the other orbs I've captured and validates the emotions I was feeling at that moment.

We captured a fantastic orb-like energy form on video on a decommissioned aircraft carrier, the USS *Hornet*, for which I may have been directly responsible. The *Hornet* is a legendary icon of World War II naval battles and saw more combat than just about any U.S. Navy ship during that war for the ages. Below decks of the carrier, just underneath the main flight deck, we set up a static night vision camera at one end of a corridor. I then used a bullhorn as a trigger object and announced "Battle Stations! Get to your battle stations!" over and over again in the hopes that any spirits on the ship would react, move, and be seen.

Minutes later, a very bright energy form, as clear as I'd ever seen, moved down the corridor toward the camera at the same pace and height as an adult human in a hurry. What was unique about this is that the more it traveled, the more it spiraled into a luminescent charged energy form. It had its own light and had a strange twisting motion like a miniature tornado. Was this the spirit of a sailor reacting to the call to arms? The orb moved with a sense of urgency, like a man in battle would, and when you combine that with the trigger object, it makes for a great piece of paranormal evidence.

But the best orb evidence I've ever captured was at one of the most profoundly evil places I've ever been: Poveglia Island in Italy. The island was witness to thousands of deaths over the course of its very dark history, which I will get into later. For now, I just want to focus on the orb that passed in front of my EMF detector and registered a reading higher than I ever thought possible.

We had just gotten started on the investigation and were in the main hospital where hundreds of people had perished. I was doing a regular sweep, asking the normal baseline questions when my EMF detector suddenly spiked. But this wasn't just an ordinary spike from 0 to 2 milliGauss, which would be impressive by itself. This time it went from 0 all the way up to 26 milliGauss! That's a huge difference and a jump in electromagnetic energy like I had never seen before and have not seen since. I was shocked because the moment something like that happens, it's mind blowing. Even a seasoned investigator like me takes a moment to absorb what's happening.

But what made this fascinating was something we caught later while reviewing the video footage. An orb, moving very quickly, passed in front of my EMF detector at the exact moment that the spike occurred. It was a round ball of light, just like all the others I've seen over the years, and just as it passed in front of my EMF detector, the detector spiked up to 26. Trying to debunk this orb as something natural falls apart when you add the incredible spike in EMF at the same time it happened.

It's a clear causal relationship between orbs and EMF and is probably the most definitive piece of evidence linking the two together that we will take credit for capturing.

Orbs always appear just before or during other paranormal activity, so I believe they are spirits gathering energy from our equipment or us as they try to manifest. Most of us think of apparitions as being fully clothed people, and many times they are. But really we have to think of orbs as partial apparitions in themselves.

Here's a message to you skeptics—linking orbs to higher amounts of EMF is an important step forward in paranormal science and we need to further dissect these phenomena. I get frustrated with skeptics because no matter how good the evidence is, all they want to do is point the finger at the believers and ridicule us for our beliefs. They want an apparition to sit down on a chair and make a turkey sandwich, and even if such a thing were to happen, they still wouldn't believe that it's real. They don't understand the range of evidence outside the full-bodied apparition or the crystal clear EVP. We need to stop pointing fingers at each other and have a dialogue, because we all seek answers to the same questions. I've encountered enough orbs now that I have no other choice but to accept that they are in fact paranormal. But does that mean orbs are the intelligent remnants of a deceased person? The presence of intelligence adds a whole new layer to the paranormal.

Intelligent Hauntings

I believe orbs can be either residual energy or intelligent spirits. If orbs and light anomalies reacted directly to human prodding (i.e., answering a question or moving an object on demand) then we could classify them as intelligent hauntings, but truly intelligent hauntings provide an interaction on a higher level than an orb. An intelligent haunting is just as it sounds—a spirit who is aware of its surroundings and (usually) its situation. Sometimes a spirit knows that it's dead and its spirit has remained in the physical plane, but other times it doesn't know. An intelligent haunting is a spirit that maintains its identity, memories, and personality after death. They can be good, bad, virtuous, benevolent, mischievous, evil, or just lonely.

Intelligent hauntings range from the wandering, confused spirit who can't figure out why someone is sleeping in its bed to a completely aware spirit who purposefully avoids moving on to the afterlife for personal reasons. I assume that every spirit I encounter is intelligent and deserves the recognition and respect of dealing with someone who is alive and healthy. I ask leading questions in the hopes of getting intelligent responses on my digital recorder, though I've actually heard them with my own ears at times. Getting clear responses to questions, especially when we get two or three in a row, is great evidence of an intelligent haunting. At Hillview Manor in New Castle, Pennsylvania, I got just that.

Hillview Manor is yet another forgotten relic of progress and a mainstay of paranormal investigation—an architectural masterpiece that was once stunning, but now waits to be reclaimed by Mother Earth after its human creators abandoned it. For eighty years it housed the poor, the destitute, and in its final days those awaiting the cold fingers of death, much like the building does now. As a retirement home, suicide was rampant at Hillview until it was shut down in 2004. Today the Manor is a hive of ghostly activity and home to a few spirits of an intelligent nature.

Before an investigation, it's imperative for us to walk through a building to get a feel for it and to make sure we know where all the paranormal hot spots are. This doesn't just help make the investigation a success, but it's also a safety measure so we can identify the hazards of the location while there's still light. Abandoned buildings don't have to adhere to any safety codes and they always have dangerous debris, crumbling structures, and weak floors that can injure or even kill a human.

Hillview had intelligent hauntings written all over it. During a daylight recon of the Manor, a guide named Gary took us into room 101 of the hospital's east wing where he'd had a recurring encounter with a spirit. I decided to do a quick EVP session to see if it was with us.

"If there's a spirit in here, tell us what your first name is," I asked with my digital recorder rolling.

The answer was clear. "I'm Jim," a whispered voice said. You might think this was coincidence, but clearly written on the door was the name of the patient who died there—Jim Casciato. That's not just an intelligent spirit, but also one who knows its name and can be consistently found in the same place day after day.

That evening I went back to Jim's room. For some reason I got a little emotional about having established a connection with him earlier in the day, probably because he seems to me to be a guy trapped in his circumstance. I asked Jim a simple question to verify that he was still there.

"What color are your pants, Jim?"

"Blue," he responded. Jim was indeed known to wear blue pants when he was alive. Jim's spirit showed a high level of intelligence; a ghost that still retains its identity and knows who it is after death, even if it doesn't know it has actually died.

Jim's situation underscores a basic question in paranormal science—does a person have to know he or she is dead to move on? If a person dies so suddenly that he never saw it coming and therefore doesn't know he's dead, does his spirit wander the Earth in limbo until he comes to the realization that he's no longer among the living? This is a prevailing belief among paranormal investigators. If that is true, then Jim is unaware that he's taken his last breath. He may be an innocent spirit still residing in the room where the attendants of Hillview Manor cared for him.

When terminally ill people die, they experience the process of breaking down over time. They are sick and know their time on Earth is limited so they have the time to prepare for their fate. In my opinion, they are aware they're dead, so trying to make contact with them or thinking I'll see them in their old house isn't feasible because they've moved on. Sudden, traumatic death is different. Many believe that spirits ripped from life continue to go about their daily activities as they knew them, which results in what we call "hauntings." These spirits need help.

I believe this was the case in another part of Hillview Manor. I was walking through the hospital trying to make contact with the spirits using the spirit box. The spirit box hops across frequencies at a very high rate of speed to provide white noise for ghosts to make contact on. Nick and I were having some success in the hallways when a spirit suddenly asked me for a favor.

"I got a question," a female voice said.

"Go ahead, ask," I responded.

"Let us . . . hear," she said. The voice sounded pained, like she was asking me to listen to her. I was happy to oblige.

"What's your name?" I asked.

"Alicia," she responded. I was shocked, but just as quickly as she appeared, she suddenly went quiet again. It was a great moment. I had a conversation with a female ghost who was in pain, possibly because she did not know she was dead, and wanted to be heard. I think it's also possible that we gave her enough closure to cross over because she disappeared so fast. I felt like we connected and helped her through the spirit box device. This is when the spirit box became more valuable to me. It allowed me to make contact with Alicia and possibly ease her suffering.

One of my biggest goals as a paranormal investigator is to find out what your surroundings look like after you cross over. When you're trapped inside the Hillview Manor, which was built in the early twentieth century, is all the décor the same as it was when you died? Are there record players? Are there other ghosts of your era? Or are the spirits seeing the same things we see in the physical world? What does the world look like from the other side? When we come walking through their domains with cameras, flashlights, and backpacks of strange equipment they've never seen or used, what are they thinking? Are they frightened of us or are they used to it in places like this where paranormal investigators frequently poke around? Do they see flashes of us like we do of them? Why does it seem that they can always see us but we can't see them? Do they exist in two different time eras at once?

Out of all the fictional paranormal movies I've seen, the one that I respect the most is *The Others* with Nicole Kidman. I think it accurately depicts a situation where spirits still residing in their own home do not know that they're dead. They become confused by the living, which keep passing through them, and it takes an intervention by older spirits to make them realize what has happened. It's an intriguing situation.

Let's say someone dies in a house and the spirit remains inside. Then, fifty years later, another person dies in the same house and also haunts it (such is the case of the Ancient Ram Inn). Do the spirits from both time frames all reside in the same plane or do they exist in different planes where they can't see each other? Does a separation of time of death mean a separation on the other side or are they all wandering about the house like old friends?

I believe these spirits interact with each other and have some evidence to support it. At Loretta Lynn's plantation in Hurricane Mills, Tennessee, we captured a spirit of a Civil War soldier threatening what we believe to be the spirit of someone who passed away many years later. At Ashmore Estate in Illinois, we caught an EVP of a spirit arguing with another one. Something tugged on my leg and at the same time a voice said, "don't you dare touch him." It's these moments that make me believe that the souls of the dead not only see each other, but interact socially just as we do.

I think they exist in the same plane instead of being layered over a bunch of interdimensional time zones. It's fascinating to think that a ghost from the Wild West can be sitting next to a ghost from World War II and another from just a few years ago.

Residual Hauntings

Residual hauntings are not the same as intelligent hauntings and are one of the phenomena that have mystified paranormal investigators (and quantum physicists) for decades. Residual hauntings are a moment in time that seems to play itself out repeatedly, like a broken record that skips over and over again. Residual hauntings are usually more nondescript than intelligent hauntings. A residual haunting can be anything—a car crashing into a tree, a woman walking across a balcony, a party that happened one hundred years ago, but the music still plays in the parlor of an old mansion.

These paranormal hot spots are actually more reliable for evidence gathering than intelligent hauntings because they are moments in time that repeat themselves, so they are somewhat predictable, although I don't think they can be timed and expected. Intelligent spirits can choose to hide or ignore the living altogether, but residual hauntings don't have the free will to choose when they appear and when they don't. I believe the environment affects the coming and going of residual hauntings. Temperature, humidity, air pressure, and the electrical charge in the air are all ingredients that come together to form a residual casserole, like the lantern-carrying soldier at Castillo de San Marcos.

Situated in the oldest city in America, Castillo de San Marcos is a Spanish bastion built in 1672 to protect the city of Saint Augustine, Florida. It is the oldest masonry fort and the only existing seventeenth-century fort in North America. Its walls have seen more history and bloodshed than almost any structure on the continent, and its walkways and dungeons still echo with the voices of those who lived, served, and died there.

On one of the Castillo's upper ramparts are a series of cannons that soldiers would patrol across during all hours of the day and night to look for any suspicious activity outside the fort's walls. During the years before electricity, they would use kerosene or oil lamps, and it's believed that one soldier still roams the ramparts, lighting his lamp and doing his duty night after night. I conducted an investigation of the Castillo in 2008 and captured on film a series of events that support this claim.

I had heard a lot about Castillo de San Marcos and was not disappointed with the paranormal activity there. Voices, growls, footsteps, blasts of cold air, and orbs littered the old fort, but it was the night watchman that was really captivating. Caught by a static night vision camera, a light on the upper ramparts clearly lit, flickered for a moment, and then moved away. The actions were very reminiscent of a soldier lighting a lamp and then walking his patrol and I believe this is a residual haunting from the days when the garrison was manned by the Spanish Army. I do not believe this is the intelligent spirit of a deceased soldier, but rather a brief window into another time when troops walked those ramparts, doing their duty to ensure everyone inside was safe.

The Birdcage Theater in Tombstone, Arizona, provides another great example of a residual haunting, but with a very intriguing twist. The Birdcage's history is ripe for paranormal activity. It was a combination theater, poker hall, saloon, and brothel during the mining boom of the 1880s. It operated continuously for eight years until the silver veins dried up, the people left, and the town went with it. During its short, eight-year lifespan, it is estimated that over ten million dollars changed hands in the basement poker room, and in 1882 the *New York Times* called it "the wickedest, wildest place between Basin Street and the Barbary Coast."

There is not a lot of documented death associated with the Birdcage Theater, though many reports of ghost sightings on the main floor have been documented. What's more interesting is how hundreds of people (including me) have heard the unmistakable sounds of a poker game being played in the basement. Late at night the sounds of plastic chips hitting the wooden table, people laughing and singing, and even glasses clinking together in an old-west toast echo throughout the floor. It's a Class A residual haunting of a bygone era.

But upstairs something different is happening. The old theater and its private "birdcages," which were built so prostitutes could have a little privacy for entertaining their clients, has a platoon of intelligent spirits roaming its halls. I saw a clear apparition of a woman's face as she moved quickly through the theater, and had several other experiences with intelligent spirits on that floor.

This dichotomy of hauntings brings up a fascinating question. If there are intelligent spirits wandering the Earth in the nonphysical plane, then how can there be a moment in time that repeats itself over and over again in the same building? How can there be intelligent hauntings upstairs and a residual haunting downstairs? Do the two ever interact? Can the intelligent spirits interact with the residual ones or do they even know each one exists? How does this work?

Residual hauntings are the one phenomenon in paranormal science that may be explainable by purely natural means, but you have to open your mind a little. Quantum physics tells us that we shouldn't think of time as being linear. It doesn't have a beginning and an end and doesn't travel in a straight line. Humans only characterize it that way because we have to. Putting time in a straight line with a beginning (the dawn of mankind) and an end (present day) is the only way we can comprehend it.

The day begins and ends. We celebrate the passing of each year and we count the years to document our lives.

But in fact, some of our leading scholars on the subject say time is infinite and does not travel in a straight line. Like many things in nature, it wanders and branches out in several directions and maybe even double-backs on itself. There's almost nothing in nature that is perfectly straight. Trees grow upward in every direction to absorb light and rivers flow downhill following the path of least resistance. Quantum physics says time is the same. There are several theories that suggest time either branches out in several directions at once or flows like a river, wandering throughout the universe.

If we accept this "river theory" of time, then it's possible that time can double-back on itself and create an isolated pocket where the present and the past are in close contact, much like a salient point on a river. It's possible that today and a certain day in 1873 are separated by a thin layer of time and space, so we can find a hotspot where we can see and hear the past playing itself over and over again. This could explain residual hauntings, and it's why I think paranormal investigators and quantum physicists seek answers to the same questions. We both seem to be working toward the same goal—to understand the unexplained phenomena of the universe—and should work together to achieve it.

Sounds and Smells

The sounds of the Birdcage Theater are wonderful to experience, and they illustrate how some of the most common paranormal activity is heard, but not seen. I've had literally hundreds of incidents of door slams, footsteps, objects being dragged, and various other sounds while conducting investigations. Many times these incidents are caused by drafts, changes in barometric pressure, the cooling and settling of a building, or pipes knocking together when air or water is pumped through them. But many times none of the natural conditions necessary to cause objects to strike each other and make noise are present, which leaves no other explanation but to label it as paranormal activity. Every time I hear something out of place, I investigate it and try to debunk it. At least 50 percent of the time I find nothing that could have caused the sound.

Footsteps are very common in paranormal investigations, so much so that I expect to hear footsteps above me almost everywhere I go. They seem to happen with more regularity than other sights, smells, and sounds. At the Moon River Brewing Company in Savannah, Georgia, I was preparing for an investigation of this old building when I heard the distinct sounds of boot heels clacking on the wooden floor above. It was loud and unmistakable and I was absolutely sure someone else was in the building. Nick and I ran upstairs to see who it was and tell them to get out of the building, but no one was there. We had already been locked into the establishment for the evening and confirmed that no one else was in the building. My only conclusion is that it was the residual energy of a former worker walking across the floor and dragging something heavy, like a barrel or a chest . . . or a body.

Footsteps like these were also common during an investigation at the Vulture Mine outside Phoenix, Arizona. Once a thriving community centered on the most productive gold mine in the state's history, the Vulture Mine was a community of nearly five thousand people at one point. The mine closed during World War II, and a once-flourishing community became a cold, desolate spot on a forgotten map. At least twenty-five people are known to have died suddenly and violently in what was once Vulture City and their spirits are trapped in a lonely town with nothing but miles of open desert to keep them company . . . until I showed up.

Everywhere I went in those buildings, footsteps echoed from different rooms and floors. And these were not modern-day tennis shoes or soft-soled kicks. Those would have sounded different. The sounds were clearly hard-soled boots with heels, so it's easy to believe that they were the footwear of a past era. It was like an entire company of miners had just gotten off work and marched through the old town, but didn't want to be seen. They were as elusive as heat waves on the desert floor that you only see from miles away but not up close.

If I was in one room, the footsteps were in another. When I was on the ground floor, boots walked across the floor upstairs. When I went upstairs, they were downstairs. It was like a game to them and since it was harmless, I played along. I would rather hear footsteps all around me than nothing at all. That way, at least I know they're there and I'm doing all I can to make contact with them.

But when it comes to phantom sounds, one of the creepiest things I've ever witnessed also "played out" at the Vulture Mine. During our investigation there, Aaron distinctly heard the sounds of a piano playing in the schoolhouse. He stood motionless in the main room listening to the music, but the keys on the dilapidated piano, which had sat unused for probably one hundred years, were not moving. Beyond that, the piano was incapable of playing music. Its strings were long gone and its keys were stuck. Aaron walked over to it and pushed on several keys to make sure it wasn't capable of making sound and nothing came out of it. There was no way it could play music, yet we all heard the notes floating through the air of the abandoned building.

How does a piano that doesn't even work make music? Was this a residual haunting of a room full of miners and entertainers letting off steam after a long day in 1880? Was it a child's recital after long hours of laborious practice? I can't ascribe any intelligence to sounds like these. To me, random sounds that are not human voices, and especially footsteps, are residual hauntings. They're the echoes of prison guards still walking their beats, of miners striding over an old wooden floor, of brewery workers dragging goods from one end of the store to another, and of history that refuses to be forgotten. Whatever it was it gave us a priceless Aaron Goodwin facial expression for the books.

Smells are another part of paranormal investigation that boggles me. I've smelled horse manure in Castillo de San Marcos, and I'm pretty sure it wasn't Aaron's gas, because he doesn't eat hay. I've smelled perfume in the Old Washoe Club, a rotting corpse in my apartment in Michigan, the foul and musty air of mold at the Ancient Ram Inn, and the putrid stench of sulfur in Bobby Mackey's Music World. These smells were always out of place and had no source. It's something I love about paranormal investigation, because it takes me to the time period when the building was alive and teeming with activity. It also serves as a warning that more paranormal activity is about to happen. It's a yellow light at an intersection begging you to make a decision—slam on the brakes or floor it. I'm not big on brakes.

Like sounds, I would classify these incidents as residual hauntings, but then again they always seem to precede paranormal phenomena, so they might be the precursors to something bigger. I've heard the tales of a pipe-smoking, nineteenth-century mogul wandering the halls of his old home and a perfume-soaked prostitute stalking an old inn, so it's certainly feasible that odors can be one characteristic of an intelligent spirit that still roams its old stomping grounds. If I smell sulfur in a dilapidated barn and no one has eaten White Castle hamburgers, then bad stuff is about to happen.

The People We Meet

Just as with life, someone can be in the wrong place at the wrong time and become part of a paranormal experience, whether they want to or not. Innocent bystanders frequently get left in the wake of ghostly activity. It's one of the best parts of paranormal investigation: listening to the stories of the people who were there. Former residents, patients, caregivers, guards, workers, or inmates can unlock clues to the source of a haunting. They witnessed the weirdness as it happened and had to live or work in an environment that most people are not subjected to. They had to deal with these phenomena on a daily basis, listen to the voices that people told them weren't there, and do a self-assessment to determine their own sanity. I respect people who dealt with that and came through it. A big part of being a paranormal investigator is listening to these people and, many times, helping them cope with it.

Red Bone

One of the first people I ever met was outside Moundsville Penitentiary in West Virginia. We were filming some background footage when a little red car pulled up and an older man

I can only describe as a "character" interrupted us.

"What choo guys filming?" he asked in a backwoods drawl.

"We're making a film about the prison," I replied.

"I was in there. A lot of years."

"Mind if we talk to you about it?" He pulled his car over (I think it said "Limited Edition Escort" on it) and I was giddy at the thought of getting a guided tour from a man who was on the inside. And I mean REALLY on the inside—not an administrator or a tour guide, but someone who lived under the iron fist of justice for many years. A man who not only looked despair in the eye and didn't flinch, but someone who would turn out to have an intimate relationship with the spirits that haunted the prison. He was Tom "Red Bone" Richardson, an inmate from 1967 to 1983, and an apparent fan of ZZ Top from the looks of his flowing white beard. I really hoped that he would leave his overflowing tobacco spit cup in the car before we began.

When we took Red Bone around the prison, I was pretty quiet. Walking the aisles of steel bars and fencing built to control the movements of dangerous men, I could see the emotion in his eyes. I could feel the intensity of the life he led and see the pain in his cragged face at every turn. I tried to visualize what he saw, but of course, failed to, not having any idea what life at rock bottom is like.

I could hear the pain in his voice and when I saw him break down and cry, his emotions started hitting me as well. When he partially collapsed, I felt the hell that this guy had lived in to pay for his crimes. He was an inmate, but he was also a man who was treated like an animal in this medieval place. It was a punch to the gut for me. I felt sorry for him and got teared up. But the reason we did this is because it gave us a sense of not only what happened there, but what the spirits were going through, which set the stage for the evening's encounters.

Ray Gaughenbaugh

When we want to find people who worked in a haunted building while it was still in operation, we do it the old-fashioned way—we go knocking on doors and asking around town. It can be nerve wracking because you never know when you're going to find someone who wants to cooperate and someone who pulls out a shotgun and delivers a "get off my property" ultimatum (it's happened).

In Moundsville, West Virginia, we got a little more than we bargained for when we knocked on the door of Ray Gaughenbaugh (at first I thought his name was Golfingball). We'd been told he worked at the prison, so we stopped by his house. Ray is old, so when the door opened and he immediately fell flat on his back, it really worried me. For a moment I seriously thought he saw the cameras, fainted from fright, and died. Lucky for us, he just had a bad case of imbalance and fell over from lack of equilibrium. He ended up being a great source of information on the prison, but not before putting a little fear into us . . . and comedy.

Sarah Knight

Sarah Knight, Sloss Venue Coordinator, was well versed on the inner workings of the Furnace. She knew all the weird stories and didn't need any sort of map to get around, probably because she already had one tattooed on her lower back. It was a simple black skyline of the Furnace that was both creepy and cool at the same time. Oddly, this would not be the last time we saw something like that. For a moment I thought Sloss Furnace once manufactured humans, and she was branded with its logo. After all she was hot like the Furnace. Okay, bad joke.

Animal Hauntings

The possibility of animal spirits brings up many intriguing questions. Their very existence suggests that free will is not involved in hauntings and/or crossing over to the other side because animals do not have the consciousness to choose. If animals can stay in the physical world after death, then it would stand to reason that living beings do not have a choice when it comes to crossing over, that nature randomly chooses who will and will not remain in the physical plane.

Or it could mean that we're completely wrong when we assume that animals are not conscious beings. Do animals actually have the ability to think and choose like us? Do they possess a soul just as we do? Could animals have unfinished business and need closure like humans? Let's say for example that a loyal dog dies, but did not have the luxury of seeing its master one last time before it did. Would its spirit remain behind looking for him? Could the bond between human and animal be so strong as to keep its spirit from crossing over? The fact that most animal hauntings are of dogs, cats, and horses—the animals most associated with human relationships—suggest this might be true. It could also mean that only animals with higher brain functions become restless spirits, since stories of turtle, parakeet, and slug hauntings are virtually unheard of.

Another possibility is that we are causing the apparitions

of animals ourselves. Telekinesis might not be a popular theory, but there have been a few documented cases of it. It's very possible that we lead ourselves into believing a beloved pet is in our presence just by thinking very intently about it. People often say, "I loved that dog. I can still see him." With a little emotional stress, it's possible that we produce an image of a deceased animal with our own telekinetic energy. In this case, it's the owner's love for his or her pet that keeps its spirit alive, not the inherent nature of the animal itself. The fact that the vast majority of animal ghosts are those of beloved family pets could be an important clue that this might be the case.

I believe there are animal hauntings, but they are very infrequent and difficult to pinpoint. Animals make sounds that are easily confused with everyday sounds and it's pretty hard to have any intelligent conversation with Fluffy or Spot. While investigating the Ancient Ram Inn in England, I was told that two cats were frequently seen in the building—a large, mangy cat upstairs and a black one that had been seen roaming the main lounge. Throughout that investigation I kept hoping I would feel one of them rub against my leg or capture purring on my digital recorder, but it never happened.

I've never seen an apparition of an animal, but twice I've captured some compelling audio that suggests a dog haunting. At La Purisima Mission my digital recorder captured what sounds like a dog whining. At the Edinburgh Vaults I again captured more whining sounds, which corresponded to what many witnesses said about a dog that still roams the catacombs.

I've captured many growls on recording devices, but these are different. Growling is associated more with demonic entities than animals and is often accompanied by dark, evil energy that lurks in the crevices of the afterlife.

As cheesy as it sounds, I want to believe the paranormal world was portrayed accurately in the movie *Ghost*. I want to believe spirits of the dead roam the Earth with unfinished business looking for someone who can hear or see them, and once they find that person, they latch on. I believe there are wandering spirits who are waiting to find someone to tell their story to or who are hiding from the afterlife out of fear of what might happen to them when they cross over.

That's something I want people to know. Many spirits were either ripped from life or never lived long enough to become bitter or disillusioned by the world. They just want to feel companionship or to know that someone can hear them. And in the end, don't we all?

SECTION

III

Sadness
and Confusion

I can't imagine the deep sadness of being discarded and abandoned in a mental institution. I don't want to envision the maddening confusion of being trapped in an empty building where your only companionship is the occasional prodding paranormal investigator like me. The pain and depression of living and dying in the unforgiving sterility of a hospital bed that deprives the human spirit of its very life energy is a loneliness I never want to know. I imagine it's like being buried alive and screaming out, hoping someone on the surface hears you. It's these situations that make paranormal investigation difficult, because it becomes almost impossible to separate your own emotions from the pain and turmoil these spirits went through before they passed on. It also adds to our own confusion of wondering if we're in the presence of the spirit of a mentally insane criminal or just a confused and harmless individual.

There is a big difference between people who died suddenly and those who died knowing how desperate their situation was. The spirits who knew the end was near usually have clarity about their surroundings and know the eventuality of their lives, so they can move on. But the ones who passed suddenly can harbor a burning passion for closure or forgiveness for what happened to their physical body. You might think angry or evil spirits are the most difficult to encounter, but in fact it's the ones who either can't figure out how to cross over or the ones who still hold on to a soul-crushing sadness that are the hardest with which to interact. The angry and evil ones come at me from a known place of hate, so I know how to deal with them. The sad and confused spirits aren't sure what they want and usually need help figuring it out. They weep aloud and wander in pain until they find it. Those are the hardest ones to deal with because they tug at your heartstrings and test your humanity.

Sad Spirits

A suburb of Boston, Sudbury, Massachusetts, is one of the oldest communities in America and sits a stone's throw away from the infamous town of Salem, where nineteen people were hanged on dubious accusations of witchcraft by their own paranoid peers. Longfellow's Wayside Inn was built in Sudbury in 1707 as a combination residential house for the Howe family and a lodge for weary travelers, and has been occupied continuously ever since.

Three-hundred-year-old homes almost always have hauntings. It's rare that a building can stand the test of time like this one and not have a restless spirit or two roaming it. I went there in February 2011 because the tale of Jerusha Howe sounded like a good romantic backstory for a Valentine's Day investigation, but in fact I would leave Sudbury in almost the same state of mind as when I left Preston Castle where the restless soul of Anna Corbin touched me—only with a slight difference.

Jerusha is a case study in heartache. It started as an innocent crush and grew to an all-consuming obsession that owns her to this day. The details are lost to time, but we do know that the man she fell in love with departed Sudbury to take a journey across the ocean to England and was never heard from again. We all know that "love" is an impossibly difficult thing to find, and happily married people always say "when you've found the right one, you'll know." Imagine when Jerusha found her true love only to have him disappear. Those feelings and deep emotions were life changing, and when that love does not return for you there's nothing left to do but die from despair. Even in my favorite movie, *Bram Stoker's Dracula,* lost true love had the power to turn one into a vampire. Now, that's my kind of love.

It's said that Jerusha never loved another and even after her death she continues to wait patiently for his return. Her spirit wanders the halls of Longfellow's Inn, inquisitively gravitating toward men to see if they are her long lost suitor (what strikes me as weird about this story is that she did not find another love while she lived the last days of her sad life, but now she flirts with hundreds of men while deceased).

On quiet days Jerusha can be heard playing the piano, and on other days she reaches out to touch men as they walk by. In one room, it's believed she climbs into bed with them at night to caress them. I would joke here that Jerusha is my kind of spirit and I was looking forward to meeting her, but her plight only raised sympathy in me. Jerusha leads an eternal afterlife of loneliness that I would not wish on anyone, so I was very motivated to make contact and ease her suffering.

> *Did you know?* **This was the first time I witnessed a fetish up close and personal—the possibility of having sex with a ghost. I interviewed a big, burly guy who talked about how much he enjoyed the feeling of when "Jerusha put her arms around me in bed." Then he went on to say that his wife and he were booking the room again to possibly have "a ghostly ménage à trois." I laughed, but then the room got silent. He was serious. Wow. Um . . . okay. This is for real isn't it? Well, I'm here to document evidence, and in this case if it happens, I really can't stop it and don't know if I even want to.**

The Inn was so completely opposite from the dark, brooding places I've investigated that it took some getting used to. Instead of possessions, growls, and tales of demons, it felt more like a bubble bath, slippers, and a robe were in order. It was a comfortable, quaint cottage environment that certainly didn't seem like the place where an agonized ghost frightened (and intrigued) the residents.

Jerusha has been reported to be most active in room number nine, so I lay down on that bed and got to work. Before long I felt the unmistakable tap of fingers on my right leg and knew there was a presence in the room, not only from this physical touch, but because I felt the heavy air that always accompanies the presence of a spirit.

A wave of pure ecstasy hit me like snake venom. What may sound like just a tap to you was a transference of incredible energy that you just have to feel to understand. There's a scene in *Bram Stoker's Dracula* where Keanu Reeves is being seduced in bed by several gorgeous bloodthirsty erotic vampires and he can't do anything but sit there and be at the mercy of their trance. This wasn't as extreme as that, but it made me feel almost the same. Now if Jerusha had made herself visible, and she looked like one of those vampires, I wouldn't be typing this right now—catch my drift?

In Anna Corbin's room I felt at peace, as if she was telling me everything was going to be alright. I felt that Anna knew she was dead and did not want me to feel sad over it. With Jerusha, it was more like she was longing for the companionship of someone. I believe spirits like Anna and Jerusha want you to feel their emotions. They try to work through you like an avatar, and once you tap into that energy, it's better to talk about the emotion and make a connection with the spirit instead of opposing it (but not when you encounter an evil one).

Although it didn't happen while I was there, we captured visual evidence of a spirit in room number nine on a full-spectrum camera that we set up. As its name implies, the full-spectrum camera operates in the full light spectrum, from infrared to ultraviolet. It can see things our eyes can't and is very efficient at detecting any changes in light.

When I reviewed the footage from that camera the next morning, I was surprised at what I saw. A mist, clearly in the form of a woman, manifested next to the bed in room nine. It formed, floated for a moment, and then dissipated. It looked like a woman walking around the bed, and I knew instantly that this was the spirit who reached out to me earlier in the evening. I finally got to see the woman who touched me. I saw Jerusha Howe. Even more exciting was that just before this capture, I clearly saw with my own eyes a white dress moving toward Jerusha's room from the top of the staircase. So to have captured on film the same thing that I saw was astounding.

Jerusha's sadness stems from the longing for a loved one whose fate she never learned. Hers is a sad story, but not on the same level as another spirit I encountered who blamed himself for the accidental deaths of several people and who still wanders the Earth wracked with guilt.

The story of Jonathon Widders goes like this: In the spring of 1914 the wealthiest family in North Adams, Massachusetts, the Houghtons, invested in their first car, a huge status symbol in those days. On August 1, Mr. A. C. Houghton and his daughter, Mary, decided to go to Bennington, Vermont, for a pleasure drive of about three hours. The family's matriarch, Cordelia Houghton, stayed at home, so they were accompanied instead by Dr. and Mrs. Robert Hutton of New York.

With their longtime chauffeur, Jonathon Widders, at the wheel, the car left the mansion at 9:00 AM and by 9:30 the group was in Pownal, Vermont, heading up an inclined road. The road was under repair and partially blocked by a team of horses on the right side as their car approached. Behind the wheel, Jonathon Widders decided to pass the horses on the left at about twelve miles per hour. It would prove to be a deadly mistake.

On the narrow left shoulder the car tilted. One wheel slipped over the edge and the vehicle began an unrecoverable slide down a steep embankment. The vehicle rolled over three times before coming to rest in an upright position in a farmer's field. Everyone except Mary Houghton was thrown clear. The men all escaped with minor injuries, but Mrs. Hutton was killed almost instantly when the car rolled over her. Mary Houghton was just as badly injured and died five and a half hours later at the North Adams Hospital. Expecting to survive, Mr. Houghton was taken home, traumatized and in disbelief. The investigator for the State of Vermont cleared Widders of all wrongdoing, blaming the accident instead on the soft shoulder of the road. But Widders still blamed himself, and the next morning he took his own life in the cellar of the Houghton barn with a single gunshot to the head. Ten days later, A. C. Houghton, having lost his precious daughter, passed away in his beloved mansion.

In the basement of the Houghton Mansion I sat on an old steel chair conducting an EVP session. The mansion had been very active, and we'd captured several pieces of great paranormal evidence, but the one I was about to capture would shock me.

In the basement, I got that heavy feeling in my gut and my Spidey senses tingled, suggesting there was a spirit in the room, so I asked a few times out loud who was with me. Then I called the spirit out by name. "Jonathon Widders . . . are you here?" I didn't realize it until I listened to the recorder later, but at that moment I got a chilling response.

"Ran for help." It was a man's voice and the syllables were clear and easy to make out. This was not a muffled EVP, but rather a crystal clear statement made by the man who took his own life rather than live with the guilt of what he'd done.

I wholeheartedly believe it was the voice of Jonathon Widders explaining to me that he had run for help after the accident that claimed the lives of Mrs. Hutton and Mary Houghton. The voice was filled with regret and sadness and wasn't a simple statement of fact—it was an explanation and maybe even a plea for forgiveness. It was Jonathon Widders's admission that he tried to find help after that terrible accident.

This is why knowing the history of a building before conducting an investigation is so important. If we hadn't been aware of Mr. Widders and the accident, I don't think we would have deciphered the meaning behind this voice. I will admit that a lot of EVPs are open to skepticism because we sometimes try too hard to identify speech patterns and look too deeply into what is many times just garbled noise. But this EVP response was clear as day and represents a great example of an intelligent haunting.

Moment of Mortality Spirit

An only slightly more common yet closely related phenomenon to the living ghost is the "moment of mortality ghost" in which the manifestation of a person far away suddenly appears to a friend or family member at the precise moment of death. A woman, for example, suddenly awakens from a deep sleep and sees her father, whom she knows to be residing at a nearby nursing home, sitting on the foot of her bed. Though surprised, she is even more amazed to hear him say, "Don't worry. I'm okay," before suddenly vanishing, filling her with confusion and panic.

Finally persuading herself she has simply had a strange dream, she falls back to sleep only to be awakened a few hours later by a phone call from her mother telling her that her father passed away during the night. Recalling that her phantom visitor appeared at 2:15 AM, she asks her mother when her father passed, only to be told 2:15 AM—precisely the moment she saw him in her bedroom.

This isn't something anyone can actively investigate because we can't always predict death, but it's an intriguing part of the paranormal science nonetheless. Can we establish such powerful bonds with each other that at the moment someone dies his or her spouse or friend or family member gets a paranormal wake up call?

Shadows

Shadows (or shadow figures) are common in paranormal investigation and are the centerpiece of many reported hauntings, but they're also the culprits of false claims as well. Shadows of physical objects (especially humans) can be mistaken for paranormal activity and photokinesis (shadows moving out of the corner of your eye as a result of natural light reflecting or refracting) is oftentimes to blame for perceived ghost sightings. However, we've captured countless pieces of evidence of shadow figures that we could not debunk as photokinesis or any other phenomenon after thorough analysis, so I am a believer in shadows and shadow figures being paranormal.

We captured a great shadow at Ashmore Estates in Ashmore, Illinois. Once called the Coles County Almshouse, it was a home for the indigent, the poor, and the mentally disabled and has at least two hundred reported deaths on the property, so it's just my kind of place. During an investigation there, I was in the main stairwell. Nick was a flight above shooting down with an IR camera, and Aaron was a flight below shooting up at me with the only light source in the building. Earlier in the night I had heard a loud bang come from a room, which was also the same spot where a man had been thrown from his chair by an unseen force. So I decided to take pictures of the doorway with a full-spectrum camera in IR mode.

I took three pictures. In the first picture there was nothing but empty space around the doorframe. In the second picture the upper torso of a man could be seen creeping into the frame, as if he were curious to know what we were doing and wanted to peek into the hallway. The third picture was the jackpot. A fully formed shadow figure of a man had moved into the doorframe! I was happier than a housewife at "Oprah's Favorite Things" show.

We were able to debunk this on the spot as not being anything normal. The only light source in the house at the time was an IR light below me, which could not have projected any image in that direction. There was no way it could have been a shadow from Aaron or Nick because they were not even on the same floor at the time and both of them were holding cameras, but the shadow figure was not.

Tips for you paranormal investigators: *It's so much better to try to debunk in the moment rather than waiting until later. I noticed the shadow in the picture on the spot and ruled out any variables then and there instead of trying to re-create the situation somewhere else. Also, always take pictures in a series like I did. By taking two or three pictures from the same spot, you can eliminate false positives, matrixing, contamination, and lens flares. You can also compare pictures to see if anything is different between them, just as in this case.*

But one of the best shadows we've ever captured was during an investigation of Old Fort Erie on the banks of the Niagara River, just across the Canadian border from Buffalo, New York. To this day it gives me chills to think about it, and I only wish it had happened to me instead of to the human trigger object that we persuaded to participate in the investigation with us.

Holding a strategically advantageous location at the north end of Lake Erie, the old fort was bitterly disputed by the American and British forces during the War of 1812. It was built by British Canadian forces in the area, taken by the Americans, and then abandoned in 1813. The British reoccupied Fort Erie, but were then driven away by the Americans in 1814. Before dawn on August 15, 1814, the British launched an attack to re-take the fort, but the battle had disastrous results. The Americans had plenty of time to establish a strong defense around the fort, and when the battle was over, the British had lost over a thousand men. That event broke the British and forced them to withdraw, but just two months later the Americans were forced to abandon the fort yet again to respond to new British threats in the eastern states. Before leaving Fort Erie for good, American forces destroyed most of it to prevent anyone else from using it, which is how it remained for over one hundred years.

Reconstruction started in 1937 and lasted two years, during which time Fort Erie gave up a few of its hidden secrets. A mass grave of 153 soldiers was unearthed and a second grave of 23 soldiers was also discovered where a private residence now sits.

Did you know? *An interesting feature of these remains is that they were identified by the buttons on their coats. Up until the American Civil War most soldiers wore distinctive buttons on their coat that bore the symbol of their regiment. During the American Revolution the Delaware Regiment wore buttons with DR stamped on them. When these graves were discovered, the only way to tell which bodies were British and which ones were American were by their buttons.*

Visiting the site where these graves were discovered and unearthed was absolutely moving. As a proud American, the knowledge that a group of soldiers who served a pivotal, patriotic role in the founding of our country were dumped in a hole with no honorable burial shook me. Sitting at the kitchen table of the man who was responsible for their just and proper burial on American soil filled my body with happiness and pride.

Death was a familiar friend to the old bastion, and the paranormal activity that we expected to find there did not disappoint. There were several hot spots, but the fort's kitchen was especially intriguing. A tour guide named Daryl had experiences of being watched and had heard strange voices in the kitchen, so we decided to use him as a trigger object and see if we could entice a spirit to make contact with him. After all, he was not just some ordinary guy—his ancestors had fought at Fort Erie. But we got more than we bargained for.

We sent Daryl into the kitchen alone and in his period garb, but with video support so Aaron and I could watch him from our base. He had a digital recorder and we set up two IR cameras in the room with him. Daryl tried to make contact with whoever was there, starting with basic questions. We discovered later that a disembodied voice answered him.

"What happened?" a voice asked. Daryl did not hear it but it was captured on his digital recorder. Could this have been a soldier asking how he died? Moments afterward, Daryl saw something that he could not believe and those of us watching him on the monitors also found incredible. A black arm moved on the wall in front of him. It was clearly a right arm with four to five digits. It dangled momentarily as if someone was standing still. Then it rose up, as if to scratch its chest, and then moved away. It was so apparent that Daryl saw it with his own eyes as it happened. Even more shocking was the shape of the digits. They did not look like human fingers, but more like a claw with talons.

"Jesus Christ. What the hell was that?" Daryl said out loud. This was as clear as the shadow you and I cast on a sunny day. It was not thin and wispy and you did not have to struggle to see it in a grainy video clip. It was there and there was no denying it.

The great thing about it was the clearly distinct presence of digits. Notice that I did not say they were fingers and a thumb. At first we thought they were, but upon closer frame-by-frame investigation they looked more like long, bony witch fingers on the end of a claw. At first we thought we were dealing with something human (which you may laugh at, but just wait until I tell you the stories of nonhuman entities in the upcoming chapters), but afterward we were not sure. The arm and "hand" somehow morphed and when it came together it looked like the arm shape-shifted into some weird shape before disappearing.

Thinking that the shadow belonged to a human, we thought we could reason with it and hopefully make intelligent contact, which Daryl tried. I have to give him a lot of credit. He stood his ground and stayed in the kitchen trying to make contact when others would have been too scared to stay. Unfortunately, there was no more contact, so we left baffled by this strange shadow figure.

We assume that this was a shadow, that it was cast by a spirit in between the only light source in the room and the far wall. But if so, then how did Daryl see the shadow and not the spirit casting it? Also, how did Daryl see a shadow from an infrared light source since he can't see the infrared light spectrum? What you have to remember is that there was no visible light in the room at the time. The shadow was being cast from the infrared light of the camera in the corner, so it's odd that Daryl saw it happen in real time.

Unless it was not a shadow?

It's possible that the arm itself was an apparition that manifested and then disappeared. This is where paranormal investigation (and physics) gets tricky. The arm was solid and black and had all the qualities of a shadow, but it's also possible that it was something else. It could have been a spirit who only had enough energy to partially manifest and could not show his entire body. The spirit might not have been able to form into a full person, but had enough energy to form an arm for a few brief seconds. This happens frequently, and in fact, it's rare to see the entire body of an apparition.

It could have also been a residual haunting of a cook preparing a meal in the kitchen back in 1814. Residual hauntings are fascinating paranormal hot spots where history repeats itself over and over again, which this might have been. Residual hauntings usually manifest as sounds, as they do in the Birdcage Theater, so this would be a monumental discovery if we captured a visual residual haunting. Whatever the explanation, this was a shocking piece of paranormal evidence that I probably can't do justice to in words. It was fantastic and I feel privileged to have been there when it happened.

In the bigger picture, shadows like the ones at Fort Erie and Ashmore Estates are significant because spirits should not have enough mass to cast one. All of our evidence about spirits leads us to believe that they are not solid beings. They should be ethereal and resemble smoke more than they do anything tangible. So how can they cast a shadow? How can they block out light if they are gas like entities? Maybe they are really solid apparitions that are mostly invisible to us, like infrared light is undetectable by the human eye. Maybe ghosts are like paper and our infrared light source is the invisible marker that illuminates them.

I have heard and seen spirits manifest as a human form and block light behind them, but never known one to generate enough mass to cast a shadow from an infrared light until now. This is why investigating the paranormal is addicting and the most thrilling adventure life can offer. The more evidence you discover, the more questions you develop and the more answers you seek.

Mists

Like shadows, mists are one of the most common pieces of evidence in paranormal investigations. However, they're oftentimes mistaken for being spirits when they're not and therefore they must be intently scrutinized. Many natural occurrences can be mistaken as an ectoplasm mist—smoke, condensation, evaporation, steam, breath, and light reflection are a few examples (mists are sometimes called ectoplasm mists, which is a generic term for any unknown physical substance attributed to a haunting, but mostly photographic and video evidence of mists and vapors captured during ghost investigations). In my opinion, when paranormal-related mists form, this is a visual representation of the spirit's composition. It's also a partial manifestation of the pinnacle of paranormal visual evidence, the full-bodied apparition.

At Houghton Mansion, we took many pictures on each floor with an infrared camera. I like this piece of equipment because it can see in a light spectrum that the human eye cannot, so it's like having X-ray vision. At the Houghton Mansion it worked like a charm and captured a very compelling picture of a mist that had a semihuman form. Many times mists are amorphous (having no discernable form), but this one did, which got me excited. It had a shoulder and a head and was transparent.

What corroborated the photo was an accompanying temperature drop in the room. The temperature had been holding steady at 76 degrees throughout the evening (our camera had a thermometer on it and recorded the ambient temperature on each picture). But at the exact moment I snapped the photo of the mist, the temperature dropped to 64 degrees—a change of 12 degrees. On the next photo, it returned to normal. It is believed that spirits absorb energy to manifest and when they do this, the temperature drops in their immediate vicinity. This photo and the 12-degree drop in ambient temperature supported that theory.

The mist itself was a great piece of evidence, especially because of its shape, but the addition of a second data point—the temperature drop—made it more credible. Any time you can find a connection between one piece of paranormal evidence and a second piece, it increases the likelihood of the phenomenon being paranormal.

Mists must be debunked as quickly and thoroughly as possible. Taking several photos at once is one technique to ensure you're not capturing a perfectly natural event. By snapping photos rapidly, you can see the mist form and dissipate in subsequent pictures and therefore discount claims that it was already there or was a camera malfunction. A series of photos will also help you determine the origin of a false mist; for example, a radiator heater in an old house that gives off steam.

One of the best mists we ever captured was at the Linda Vista hospital in Los Angeles. Linda Vista is one of the most active places I've investigated and is the definition of creepy. It almost challenges you to come inside and be the same person when you leave.

During the night at Linda Vista, a static night vision camera set at one end of a corridor caught a mist walking down the hallway away from it. It was very clear and happened at nearly the same time we had an encounter with a full-bodied apparition in the same vicinity.

The mist was free floating so it could not have been something attached to or caused by the walls. Using the doors in the hallway as a reference, we determined that the mist was five feet tall and generated its own light in a luminescent haze. Immediately before the mist was captured, Nick saw the apparition of a female patient staring at him and our cameras froze up the same way they do when they receive a sudden surge of EMF. Multiple data points and connected pieces of evidence are the best way to corroborate paranormal activity, and this mist gave us plenty of evidence to work with.

We brought in a video specialist and tried to debunk it as light reflections, but there were no windows on that level of the old hospital. No exterior lights were present and even if there were, nothing was moving. It could not have been a flashlight or we would have seen the shadows of the chairs, cameras, or tripod cast down the hallway. In essence, we ruled out all man-made light sources.

Just like a residual haunting, I feel that the conditions have to be right to capture an ectoplasm mist or a truly paranormal being. The climate, humidity, moon phase, energy source, portals, and any other variable that we don't understand have to be in place and in the right sequence. It's like the numbers of a combination lock being in line, and once they are, we get a peek into the world beyond. When spirits have these variables in line and an energy source, they appear and disappear as quickly as a flash of lightning in the desert, so discovering the conditions that allow them to manifest is a huge step toward communicating with them.

It's one of the reasons paranormal science still involves a lot of guesswork—we still do not fully understand the conditions that need to be present for paranormal activity to occur. Once we do, though, we'll be able to accurately predict when spirits will appear and might even be able to use that small window to communicate with them. Imagine the things we will learn when that day comes.

Did you know? *While filming at Linda Vista hospital, we may have discovered more than we bargained for—actual human ash in the old incinerator. During an interview with the property's caretaker, Syd Schulz, we opened part of the crematory and found a bed of ash complete with fragments of bone or teeth. I sifted through it with my fingers and then came to realize it was the real deal.*

The Different Types of Cameras

For most people, seeing is believing. We are visually oriented people and everyone wants to capture proof of the paranormal on film because it's the most compelling medium. But what cameras should you use and what are the differences?

First off, don't discount your run-of-the-mill digital camera as not being good enough for an investigation. Simple digital cameras are uncomplicated and many times successful, especially when using its internal flash. Larger SLR digital cameras are sometimes too "smart." They try to determine light, distance, aperture, f-stop, and other variables and will actually refuse to take a picture if the settings aren't right. The benefit of these cameras, though, is the ability to take several photos in a second. This is advantageous when a spirit tries to manifest and you need to snap a series of pictures as it happens.

Night vision video cameras are a must because almost all paranormal investigations take place at night and being able to see through the darkness is key to gathering evidence (and is good for safety). Infrared cameras, like the one we used in

Houghton Mansion, are great and give fantastic results, but they're expensive. The highest order of camera for this line of work is the thermal camera, but they're very expensive and probably aren't necessary unless you're a serious investigator.

One of the most common questions I get is why do we investigate at night? My answer is because at night infrared cameras can see in a spectrum that we cannot. Investigations are not only conducted at night because that's the most likely time period to see ghosts, but because at night we can use our technology to see the other side of the visible light spectrum.

The infrared camera is a great tool. Before snapping the picture of the mist in Houghton Mansion, we took several baseline photos (also called control photos), which are very important because establishing a baseline gives us something to compare an extraordinary photo to. For example, if we think a piece of furniture moved, we can go back to our control photos to see where the item was when we first entered the house and compare them. At Houghton we snapped several pictures of that room, but the mist was only visible in one of them.

Connecting with History

I believe too many people today allow themselves to get caught up in technology and lose their connection to the people and history around them. We get consumed by the present and forget the past that led us up to this point. We tweet, Facebook, text, and make YouTube videos instead of reading and exploring. I think technology and progress is critical to a society, but

I also love to leave all of it behind and get connected with the past during an investigation.

I like to let the location speak to me, so I frequently sit still and try to feel what the buildings and land are saying when I first arrive on a site. I'm not saying that I'm a psychic, but what I will say is that somehow I have developed a sense and a feeling for a location's history. Unlike opening a textbook and reading the history, in some other way I can feel it. I think the energies of the past still remain and your body can pick up on them.

Without knowing the history of a place, you're interviewing someone with earplugs and blinders on. You have to become them and get to know them. It's cool to think that spirits may be able to add words to the history books. Through paranormal investigation and communication with the souls of the deceased, you can add unwritten pages in history books through the voices that lived it. If you know what they went through emotionally then you're putting your body and soul on the same historical plane with them. You are calibrating yourself to their time and spiritual energy. By knowing the history you can develop ways to get better evidence. You can think of paranormal investigation as a metal detector and the history is the battery. Without history to power you, finding treasure is nearly impossible.

La Purisima Mission in California is a great example of this. It was a vortex of historical energy and is easily the most spiritual place I've ever investigated. Located in the idyllic (and wealthy) central California community of Santa Barbara, the Spanish built La Purisima in 1787 specifically to convert indigenous Indians (mostly Chumash) to Catholicism. Catholic Missions like this were rampant throughout the western half of America during the eighteenth century, the most famous of which is The Alamo in present day San Antonio, Texas. In California, La Purisima is the only fully restored mission from this era still standing.

Walking the dusty grounds of the mission, I drifted off by myself more than any other investigation. While wandering on my own, I spent some time noticing the little things and had flash images of the way it was when the Indians lived there. I could see them laughing, playing, interacting, and doing the things we all envision a happy family doing. Then I see the conflict, the violence, and the epidemics introduced by the Spanish. I could see their battles and feel their suffering. We don't read about the history of a place like this in a textbook. We come here and communicate with the history. The history is not dead. The history is still alive in another form.

Inside the mission, I really feel that I tapped into the emotional turmoil of the Chumash being persecuted by the Spanish during their religious zeal to convert them. I could feel the Chumash living peacefully and quietly and then suddenly being bullied until they revolted against their oppressors. I find this phenomenon happening to me more and more as my adventures go on, but at La Purisima, it was at its most profound. Probably the one thing that hit me the hardest from that investigation was the flute music.

I had been in the mission all night, trying everything to get a reaction out of the spirits said to haunt the place and gotten good results. Near the end of the night, just hours before the sun came up, I captured on a digital recorder a lengthy EVP of flute music. This wasn't just any old flute music that someone could play while sitting on a hilltop, but notes and melodies of a long lost time that seemed to come from an instrument of a past era. It also wasn't the sound of a modern aluminum flute, but more like a hollow wooden flute carved from a tree.

That haunting music plays over and over in my mind and the more I hear it the sadder I get. I'm sure the spirits of the

Chumash people are still there playing the music of their day, and it's now the soundtrack of my experience in La Purisima. It would be easy to categorize this as a residual haunting, but I don't think it was. I think it was played on purpose for me because of how we got the spirit to play it.

We used a trigger object that evening—a portable boom box that played Chumash flute music on a loop. We thought by broadcasting it, we could get the spirits to play along with us and we were right. When we turned off the boom box, the mysterious flute music continued along with the same melody as our modern music. It seemed like an intelligent response more than a remnant from 300 years ago. Something or someone heard what we were playing and decided to play along with it after we turned off the music. I was ecstatic. Paranormal author Richard Senate, who has experience with haunted locations in that area, agreed that there was a melody that continued after we turned off the music.

That whole investigation was sad and visual, but poignant as well, because there are some things I still can't put into words from La Purisima. When the sun came up I felt like I was returning to the present from a time travel. Investigations like La Purisima feel more like journeys back into the past rather than paranormal investigations and the evidence we get just enhance the experience. This investigation was one of my first ones, so rather than provide clarity on the paranormal world, it really added a new layer to it that I had yet to understand. It left me somewhat confused, but more motivated than ever to find answers. I'm lucky that I can still seek the closure I need. Not all spirits have that luxury.

Gettysburg.

Confused Spirits

Gettysburg, Pennsylvania, is one of the most haunted locations in the world, and with good reason. Eight thousand people died in this town in July of 1863 during a battle that marked one of the three most significant moments in American history. The two greatest Armies ever seen on the continent locked horns in a battle that would change the course of human history.

One of Gettysburg's casualties was Jennie Wade, a twenty-year-old seamstress who was born and raised in the same town where she fell. On the morning of July 3, 1863, Jennie was kneading dough for bread when a single bullet (called a mini-ball in those days) crashed through the house and pierced her heart, killing her instantly. It was never determined which side fired the fatal shot, but regardless, Jennie Wade became the only civilian casualty of the battle.

One hundred forty-eight years later, the house where Jennie Wade perished still stands where it was built, and paranormal enthusiasts can take a tour at all hours for a few dollars. The believers, the curious, and the skeptics all converge on this historic structure to see or hear firsthand the spirit of Jennie. Hundreds have reported seeing or hearing her in the house.

This is a dilemma of paranormal investigation—dealing with the confused mental state of the spirit with whom you're trying to make contact. For almost 150 years, the spirit of Jennie Wade has been roaming her house, unaware that a sniper's bullet killed her when she was just twenty years old. What was on her mind when she died? She was cooking bread in the kitchen on a quiet morning while there was a lull in the battle. Her lover was away fighting the war somewhere. Her parents and other family members were still asleep when she died very suddenly. So suddenly that she may not even know it. Is her mind still in 1863? Does she still see the battle, or does she see present day? Does she notice the tourists walking through her house every day? It's a perfect recipe for a confused spirit.

In the afterlife, Jennie's mind is probably still young and vivacious and has no idea what's become of her physical body, the war that consumed her, what happened to her boyfriend who went off to fight, or where her relatives are. Like the history of a location, the mental state of the subject is something that has to be taken into consideration when conducting investigations. These are the spirits who need the most help and where the lines between paranormal investigation and parapsychology become fuzzy.

I went to the house in the hopes of contacting Jennie, but knew that even if I were successful, I would have to get past her confusion to make meaningful contact. The Wade House is small and mostly made of wood. Footsteps echo off the hardwood floors and the smell of dust dominates the air.

During the investigation I was dressed as a Union soldier when a disembodied voice asked if I needed something to drink. Was this Jennie? Did she think I was her boyfriend returning from the war and needed water? This EVP told me she still thought the world was the same as the time of her death—1863.

Hours later we unearthed a bombshell. "I'm pregnant," a female voice said on the recorder. If I thought Jennie was confused before, then I was certain that she was struggling with a lot of emotions after that. If she really was pregnant at the time of her death then she was definitely someone who needed the comfort of a family to support her, which was not there. I think confused spirits like Jennie need help to be at rest. I don't think they can close a book when so many questions are unanswered.

I hope we closed a chapter in her book by listening to her.

Jennie's case also blurs the lines between intelligent and residual hauntings. I think she is an intelligent spirit living among residual activity. Spirits like her die quickly in their surroundings, but we can't see it. It's like being trapped in a video game with its own world that the characters can see, but we can't. At places like this the residual and intelligent worlds get interlaced and it takes the right combination of people and weather to make looking into their world possible.

Did you know? In the basement of the Wade House there is an effigy of Jennie—a mannequin of plastic and papier-mâché made by the National Park Service to reenact the last moments of Jennie Wade before she was buried. Her "body" has been wrapped in cloth and placed on an old wooden bed for dramatic effect. I decided that the best way to entice a spirit to make contact with me was to try a little agitation.

"Do you not like it when I do this?" I asked straddling the mannequin. Looking back, I was probably being disrespectful and I would be apologizing right now if I had not gotten the response I was looking for. Out of nowhere I was suddenly and forcefully grabbed on the ass. You did not read that last sentence incorrectly. A hand, as plain as I had ever felt, grabbed my butt cheeks and enjoyed a hard squeeze. Normally, I would be flattered by this, but I was in a dark basement with two other guys and a doll, so it startled me. I jumped off the bed like I'd been shot and ran over to the other side of the basement.

What we did not know until later when we reviewed the footage is that an orb shot from the bed toward Nick at the same moment that I jumped off of it. It was the same type of orb that we'd seen before when weird things happen and in my opinion is a consistent perpetrator of paranormal activity.

I have to admit now that it was pretty funny and I was asking for it. If it hadn't been a grab on my buttocks and instead had been a shoulder or leg grab, I probably would have reacted differently, but for several minutes afterward I could still feel the imprint of a hand on my rear end. In one way it was great paranormal evidence, but in another way it was a warning. It was the spirit of Jennie's father telling me to stop messing around and get serious.

The Human Body Is the Best Detector: Zak's Challenge to Science

The Stanley Hotel is inviting and honest. A magnificent Georgian revival hotel built in the gilded era of American castles, the whitewashed structure sits among the equally majestic Colorado Rockies, creating a first impression that overwhelms the approaching traveler with opulence and comfort. You expect to be greeted by a tuxedoed butler and a mimosa, even if you've seen Stanley Kubrick's horror masterpiece based on Stephen King's novel, *The Shining*, and know about the building's paranormal residents who never checked out.

Rarely can someone step out of life and right into the celluloid frames of a movie, but that's exactly what the experience is like at The Stanley. It's somewhat tragic that *The Shining* misrepresented the hotel's paranormal energy so badly. The spirits in the movie are dark and possessive and force Jack Nicholson to kill, which is the polar opposite of the truth. The permanent residents of The Stanley are harmless and more than likely confused and unaware they're dead instead of being homicidal maniacs that say things like, "Here's Johnny!"

I felt a connection to the history of The Stanley Hotel from the moment I stepped foot on its grounds. As I mature as a paranormal investigator, I feel myself becoming more and more aware of my surroundings everywhere I go. And not just the physical world, but the paranormal world as well. My senses have become more acute and I feel like I'm more sensitive to the presence of paranormal energy. Again, I do not claim to be psychic, but I believe that the best tool a paranormal investigator has is his (or her) body, and that it gets more in tune to the paranormal activity the more often it gets immersed in it. It's like learning a language. You can study Spanish in school, but it's not the same as being dropped off in the middle of Bogota, where you have to learn the language to survive.

I can't stress enough the importance of training your senses. What you see on TV is two-dimensional representation of a four-dimensional world that the paranormal investigator experiences. I firmly believe that the human body can detect the presence of spiritual energy better than most electronic devices.

Some would say this is pseudoscience, but I want to challenge that assertion. Why can't the body be relied upon as a detector? Why is it so easy to dismiss goose bumps and chills as a product of the mind? Why do we discount the feeling that someone is watching us as the mind playing tricks on us? I will admit that fooling the brain is possible, and I have read about the effects of EMF on the mind. I even read a medical report that suggested the doppelganger effect is caused by stimulation of the left temporoparietal junction of the brain (I would not know what temporoparietal was otherwise).

I can buy that in a setting where there are electric currents and EMFs, but what about when I'm alone in an abandoned barn in Ohio and there's nothing that could cause that stimulation? When I hear someone behind me, smell their musk, and feel their breath on the back of my neck—three senses sending me alarm signals at the same time—how is it that my brain is playing tricks on me?

I say this—after six million years of evolution, is there anything else more in tune with the planet than the human body? We grow muscles to withstand fourteen pounds of air pressure per square inch at sea level. We develop senses to detect changes in wind patterns and know when a storm is approaching. We can hear threatening footsteps approaching and feel the stares of an angry ex-girlfriend as her eyes burn a hole in our back. We have millions of nerve endings in our skin to feel our environment. In short, we evolve. We become more in tune with the world, like birds that use the Earth's magnetic field to help guide them on their long migration or mammals that can feel winter coming and prepare for hibernation. So when my body tells me there's a spirit present, I trust it.

An experience at the Stanley Hotel bolstered my confidence in the human body's ability to detect paranormal activity. We were in the hotel's carriage house and to be honest, we were having a pretty uneventful investigation. It happens sometimes. For hours I had not gotten any EVPs and had no personal experiences. The whole night was going sour, when I decided to bring in Bill Chappell (a complete skeptic) and several devices he engineered.

Bill built a double histogram that uses simultaneous thermal imagery and sonic emanations to detect any disruptions in the local EMF. The sonic waves are used the same way sonar is used to map the ocean floor and the thermal imagery detects changes in temperature. We were all standing in the hotel's carriage house when I suddenly got a hit on my body. I felt a very cold presence and the hairs on my arms and neck raised up. Everything I knew was telling me that something was with us.

At this exact moment, Bill Chappell got a reading on his instruments that something unseen was in the room and moving. On film we captured a mist move and moments later we recorded a few disembodied voices. As I moved around the room, the apparition moved with me and my body continued to register that I was not alone.

Bill not only saw this spirit move with me on his instruments, he also saw an apparition with his own eyes. It had enough mass to block out our thermal camera and trigger it to take a photo, which revealed an unexplained energy source. These three pieces of simultaneous evidence combined with the familiar feelings I had (goose bumps, heavy air, the feeling that someone was watching me) all tell me that, *yes*, my body *is* a reliable detector of paranormal energy, no matter what anyone else claims.

The Stanley Hotel is not the only time I've had scientific instruments detect something when my body did as well. At the Salem Witch House in legendary Salem, Massachusetts, I was in an upstairs room when I got a hit on my body. I felt the normal goose bumps and chills, but also felt an extreme sadness, just like I did at Preston Castle. Several young children perished in this house over the years, and I felt like someone (probably a parent) was transferring the sadness of their loss onto me. I grabbed my Mel meter and sure enough, it was registering EMF readings far above normal. The milligauss spikes were off the charts, so I knew what my body was telling me was correct. Something was there with us.

But as suddenly as the feelings and the EMF spikes came, they also went away. We immediately conducted an EMF sweep of the room and found no natural or manmade EMFs that could have caused the spikes. The trail was cold, so we quickly followed up the encounter with an EVP session, hoping that the spirit had not left. In cases like this, it's better to press forward than to leave and be happy with what you've captured. I believe in Patton's old mantra—"Attack, Attack, Attack!"

Moments later I got a class A EVP of a man's voice that said, "Don't go in there." Even better, the disembodied voice had a Northeast accent! It dropped off the *R* in "there" like a Bostonian would.

In baseball terms, it was like batting for the cycle or pitching a perfect game. In one room I got cold, felt the emotion of the spirit, had a spike on the Mel meter, and captured an EVP all at once. It was a case study in detection that I will put up against any skeptic any day.

I'm not suggesting that anyone is capable of detecting spirits with his or her body just by going into a cold, dark room and feeling around. Sometimes people who haven't done this before can psych themselves up too much and mistake a natural cold pocket of air for something paranormal. Looking back on some of my earliest investigations, I am probably guilty of this. The only thing that attunes an investigator to his environment is time. I have been on over a hundred paranormal investigations and have gotten to the point that my senses are trained, which only comes with a lot of experience. Many times I can tell when there's something otherworldly with us and when there's nothing at all. Being sensitive is something you have to grow into and something you have to learn to work with. I am comfortable calling myself sensitive after all the investigations I've endured.

It's like a Montana fishing guide who looks at a river and immediately knows whether he's going to catch anything by the water's height, the current's speed, the activity of insects on the waterline, the weather, cloud cover, and the time of day. His eyes are trained to see the river for more than what everyone else sees. He can feel the environment above and below the water and knows exactly where to go and how to cast for pay dirt. I've known a few investigators who are like this, and their experiences are invaluable.

As unlikely as it seems, I actually look to Mixed Martial Arts for inspiration when training myself for a paranormal investigation. Professional fighters train their bodies and minds on several different disciplines. Wrestling, Muay Thai kickboxing, Brazilian jiu-jitsu, and Western boxing have proven to be the dominant forms of fighting, so MMA fighters have to train themselves in each of those techniques.

In that same way, I train my senses—sight, smell, hearing, feeling, and even taste—to detect the presence of paranormal energy. Since I was a kid I knew I was detecting things other people weren't, but I never knew what those were until now. I try hard to put myself into the era I'm investigating. I study the history, talk to the locals, and listen to the music of the era (like Chumash flutes). I almost use my body like the DeLorean from *Back to the Future* so I can time travel back to the time frame that I'm investigating.

Zak's Favorite Detector: The Mel Meter

I don't like clichés but "necessity is the mother of invention" is very true in the case of my friend Gary Galka. Gary was never a believer in the paranormal, but now he spends much of his time inventing device after device designed to communicate with the afterlife. I love the RT-EVP Real Time EVP device, but the Mel meter is my favorite. Before I tell you why, you have to hear the story of how it came to be.

In 2004, Gary's seventeen-year-old daughter was driving home when she lost control of her vehicle and slammed head-on into a tree. Four days later, the Galkas were forced to take her off of life support and watch her heart beat for the last time. Her name was Melissa.

That day they started having experiences at home. They smelled her perfume. The doorbell rang for no reason. The TVs in the house changed channels by themselves. The stereo would turn on when no one was around. These experiences were not limited to one spot in the house and soon shifted to more personal moments. The entire Galka family (they have two other daughters) kept feeling kisses, touches, and hugs and heard Melissa's voice around the house. The youngest daughter even saw an apparition of Melissa brushing her hair two separate times. One night Gary and his wife felt Melissa climb onto their bed and lie down between them at the same moment.

Overall, Gary estimates that they had around seventy encounters with the spirit of their beloved daughter in their home, and this helped them to heal and move forward. The Galkas then began to reach out to other bereaved parents who had lost children. He tried to show them there's a light at the end of the tunnel and the pain is a surmountable obstacle. The Galkas wanted to help more people, but there was only so much they could do.

A test and measurement engineer with over thirty years of experience, Gary decided to come out of retirement and do something to help. His profession in life was to solve problems and make manufacturing businesses more efficient. He would visit factories and identify friction points in their production processes and help them become more streamlined.

After watching one of the paranormal shows on TV, he saw the same thing—a need for more efficient and streamlined equipment. So he created a line of products that helped him communicate with Mel and helped the paranormal community take a huge leap forward. In honor of his daughter, he called his device the Mel-8704. The 87 stands for the year she was born, and 04 is for the year she passed to Spirit.

The Mel meter is the only multipurpose tool designed specifically for paranormal use and does more than any plain EMF detector can do. It operates between 30 and 300 hertz, which avoids broadband frequencies used by CBs, walkie-talkies, and cell phones. The Mel-REM, which is what I use, also has an antenna that radiates its own independent EMF at a different frequency that does not interfere with the main component itself.

This allows the Mel meter to measure disturbances around the antenna. When it senses an interruption, the field around the antenna collapses and triggers audible and visual LED lights that correlate to the amount of distortion in the field. The antenna is not influenced by anything within the environment unless it comes up to the antenna and has conductive properties. So it won't go off if you get a phone call or put it next to a breaker panel or a fuse box. The Mel meter is compatible with AC and DC EMF.

So in a nutshell, it can't be tricked like regular EMF detectors.

In the movie *Ghost,* what is the most frustrating element of Patrick Swayze's character? It was the living not being able to hear or see him and not being able to move things. How sucky would it be to be trapped in a world where you can't get anyone's attention? If there was a device that you only had to wave your hand in front of for the living to hear you, then that's a breakthrough. The Mel meter's antenna does that.

To add to its appeal, the Mel meter has a very accurate ambient thermometer and a red flashlight that doesn't interfere with night vision. It's like the Swiss Army knife of paranormal meters and I'm so grateful that such a talented individual decided to take action and use his skills to further the science of paranormal investigation. You can spend a lot of time in an empty room trying to find spirits and get nothing even when they're there. But with a Mel meter, it's like an eyeball for a blind investigator.

This might sound like a product plug, but the reason I bring it up is to show that the paranormal community is using state-of-the-art equipment and not Radio Shack transistors to achieve our goals. The Mel meter is a high-quality device with internal shielding, gold contacts, a brass tripod mount, and the best parts to ensure its accuracy in EMF detection. Despite that, Gary kept the price reasonable and continues to donate a percentage of the Mel meter proceeds to grief counseling organizations like Compassionate Friends. For him, it's about helping loved ones communicate with each other, even if they exist in different planes.

Electromagnetic Fields

I've talked about EMF a few times already, but what exactly is it and what is its relationship to paranormal activity? Electromagnetism is defined as one of the four fundamental interactions of particles in nature. The other three are gravity, the strong interaction, and the weak interaction—also known as the strong and weak nuclear forces.

Electromagnetism is the force that causes the interaction of electrically charged particles in our world, which takes place in an electrically charged field. Other than gravity, nothing affects our existence more than electromagnetism. Electric fields, electric currents, generators, motors, batteries, transformers, magnetic fields, magnets, and the magnetosphere that surrounds the Earth are all forms of electromagnetism. It's the force responsible for holding electrons and protons together in atoms, so it's a building block for molecules and all life as we know it.

If there's one constant relationship in paranormal research it's the connection between EMF and spirits, either intelligent or residual. Almost every time paranormal activity happens, there is an increase in EMF, so it's imperative that we understand how it works with spirits and their energy. The leading theory is that ghosts emit electromagnetic energy and cause spikes in electromagnetic fields (EMF). The common belief is that they gather energy in and send EMF out. So there is a directly proportional relationship between spirits and EMF and a simultaneous inversely proportional relationship between spirits and available energy.

As paranormal activity goes up, EMF also goes up and available energy goes down. This is a core principle of all paranormal research.

The tricky part about EMF, though, is its interaction with the human brain. Electromagnetic fields affect our perception, as does infrasound and seismic activity (just before an earthquake, millimeter waves are often released from the Earth's crust that cause us to feel disoriented and nauscous). EMF has been associated with causing sensations of disorientation, fear, nausea, and the feeling that a presence is in a room with you. I believe people can sometimes find themselves in a high EMF (sometimes called a "Fear Cage") and get the feeling that they're not alone when in fact they're caught in a high EMF and being tricked by it. So it's possible to blame spirits for something that's perfectly natural.

But fear not, paranormal investigators, there are ways to ensure you're not being duped. EMF detectors and K2 meters are your best defense. They're essential to paranormal investigation, so if you're conducting one without these key pieces of equipment, stop now and get one. But like any piece of equipment, it's worthless without a trained operator. An EMF detector that spikes in a dark room is just the first part of the puzzle. You have to look around at the other environmental factors to see what it means. Are there power lines or plumbing in the room that could be causing the spike? Is there a nearby power plant? How about a deep water well? What sort of materials is the building made of? Are you investigating an active building where people work or an abandoned farm in the middle of nowhere that has no electricity? These background questions have to be answered before you can interpret an EMF spike as being paranormal or not. Sometimes it is and sometimes it isn't.

A second or third electronic device can corroborate your evidence as truly paranormal when an EMF detector spikes. Capturing a disembodied voice on a digital recorder at the same time that a K2 meter jumps can provide a direct connection between EMF and spiritual activity. The teddy bear in the Edinburgh Vaults was a three-part event. My EMF detector spiked, a disembodied voice was caught on my digital recorder, and the bear moved all at the same time. That's golden. The point to remember is that EMF is a naturally occurring force of nature. Just because you detect it does not mean there is paranormal activity and should not be relied upon by itself to indicate the presence of paranormal beings. But tying an EMF spike to a second piece of evidence helps prove that a ghost truly is present.

Breezes That Pass Through Us

A three-hundred-pound wrestler slams you with a two-handed shove. That's what it felt like when I was assaulted by an ice-cold blast of air where there was no natural way it could have happened. Breezes are phenomena that can't be recorded by any man-made measuring device (yet), but I believe are a sign of paranormal activity. Having your body blasted by a momentary pocket of air where there shouldn't be any is frequently paranormal. I love when these hit me during an investigation because just like goose bumps, they tell me that spirits are present. These experiences are just as good as any form of visual or audio evidence of paranormal activity.

Moments like this are nearly ironclad verification that a spirit is present, but should not be taken lightly. These breezes are the physical form of a spirit that could just be passing by you, but they could also be trying to do you harm. It's possible that the spirit is so enraged by your presence that it is trying to kick, punch, or tackle you, but all you feel is a cold breeze.

I was once walking through the lower level of an old building where almost no air circulated when a powerful blast of air assaulted me. It felt like someone turned an ice-cold turbo jet onto my body at the same time that a train slammed into me. It lasted a mere second and happened at the same moment I captured several disembodied voices, unexplained knocks, and even a pair of growls. I was in a completely enclosed underground room with only one doorway. The air was stagnant, as undisturbed as it probably was two hundred years before. There was no possible natural air current or other source for what I felt.

The good thing about a blast of air is that it's easy to debunk. When it happens, I look for anything that can cause air movement or a change in air pressure—an open window, open door, a vent, a return air vent, a door that opens on one side of a building when a different door is closed—anything. Obviously breezes are not as reliable as paranormal evidence when they happen outdoors. But when you're indoors, or even underground in an enclosed room, and a blast of air that lasts only one or two seconds drives through you like a linebacker, it's a great indicator of paranormal activity.

They're also the most difficult to prove as being paranormal. As I said before, a lot of things can cause a sudden gust of air, so you have to make a superhuman effort to find the source of the breeze and eliminate contamination before chalking it up as paranormal. I do not know if carrying a barometer that measures air pressure would detect breezes like these, but it's possible. The difficulty in that is breezes are very unpredictable and only happen on rare occasions. Equipment is one of the things that always helps me stay focused during an investigation. Like a pilot in a storm who loses visual references and has to rely on his gauges, I look to my Mel meter, digital recorder, video camera, and EMF detector to help me keep my way. I trust these devices to help me gather evidence. I would drop a trail of breadcrumbs, but we all know how that tale ends.

Stay Focused

Here's a learning point for all you aspiring ghost adventurers. The investigation at Castillo de San Marcos was a learning experience for me. We all experienced multiple touches, voices, growls, and general nervousness. The activity in the dungeons was constant and is one of the few times I felt very uneasy during an investigation. We went into the dungeons hoping for one or two bits of evidence, but got bombarded with unexplained phenomena. It was the first time I had so much paranormal activity that I had to stop, get my bearings, and focus on the task at hand.

But that's what you have to do as a paranormal investigator. You have to keep your wits and stay on course to find answers. You may find yourself in a situation where you have too much paranormal activity. When other people run, we stand our ground. It's almost like an airplane crashing and the stewardess in your head is saying "everyone remain clam." It's cheesy, but good advice.

Tormented Spirits

Does the sanity of a person matter after death? If you were mentally ill in life, are you still mentally ill in death? I never thought to ask these questions until I spent some time in rural New Jersey.

Ninety acres of creepiness connected by five miles of underground confusion. That's how I'd describe Essex County Hospital. It's not just a huge complex of interconnected brick buildings; it's a mini-city that reminds me of a medieval Camelot built with the intent of closing the front gate and waiting out a long siege. That or a leper colony whose patients were stowed away behind high bushes and electric fences so as to not be an eyesore on society. When you hear the stories of neglect that happened here, it's easy to see why Essex was looked at like an ulcer on the face of an otherwise peaceful New Jersey community.

The chasm between haves and have-nots in America was never wider than during the Great Depression. Middle class families sunk into poverty while the wealthy found new opportunities to stay afloat and maintain their status. Against this backdrop, the number of patients at Essex soared. Families with status were shamed by having a mentally ill member and the everyday family simply could not afford to feed everyone. In both cases, the mentally ill and perfectly healthy were dropped on Essex's doorstep like discarded toys that had worn out their use. The emotional torment of being left alone in the company of the truly insane must have been an abyss of sadness, especially for those who were not ill at all.

During the 1950s when mental health was still an inexact

science, shock treatment, lobotomies, and water therapy (which look more like torture techniques by today's standards) were the norm. It's believed over ten thousand people died in this facility from neglect, exposure, failed experimental treatments, and complacency. That number still blows me away when I think about it, and I had to have my tour guide repeat that number to be sure I heard him correctly.

Essex ceased all operations in 2007 (just one year before our investigation) and was abandoned so quickly that personal items still littered the rooms as if a military invasion was coming and everyone dropped their utensils in the middle of dinner and fled the scene. One of the things that struck me at Essex was the colorful murals decorating the walls. But these weren't the type that lighten the mood of the place and make you feel welcome. Most of them were painted by the hands of chemical abusers and the truly insane, so their dark depictions gave the casual passerby a window into the minds of the hopeless. They littered the hallways and watched your every move as if they knew something you didn't. It was a torrent of leftover emotions and a great environment for those seeking paranormal answers like me.

The hospital had the largest volume of recorded paranormal encounters of anywhere I'd been at that time. There were literally hundreds of experiences that intrigued me from voices at night to daylight manifestations. Places like this get me charged up, but in a different way than their darker siblings. I don't feel like I'm going in there to fight with the spirits like at Bobby Mackey's or Moundsville Penitentiary. The only evil entities here were the administrators of the hospital—the ones who kept the patients subjugated and oppressed. On one ward of the hospital, eighty patients were cared for by two orderlies and many spent their days locked in a crib covered in their own feces and urine. Just researching the historical videos and seeing the conditions they lived in was disturbing.

At Essex it seemed like the buildings themselves moaned, like a rickety structure that sways from side to side and then settles in on itself, only with a human voice. At times I felt like Jonah in the belly of the whale listening to the groans of our beastly host. The bricks and mortar told us of their agonizing stories by releasing some of the countless cries of pain that had echoed down the hallways over the past hundred years.

I had several paranormal encounters at Essex, but never got the impression that the spirits there were malevolent or mean. I felt that they were the same way they were in life—confused and sad, maybe even mentally challenged, which again brings up the question of whether or not we cross over with our identities intact. If a person can pass away and still retain their personality and their experiences, then it stands to reason that they would behave the same way they did when they were alive.

If Jerusha still roams the halls of Longfellow Inn agonizing over her lost lover and Jonathon Widders still haunts the Houghton Mansion telling people what he did in those critical minutes after the fateful car accident, then it's possible that mentally ill patients still spend their final days lying in agony, waiting to be taken care of at Essex County Hospital.

I'm assuming that the paranormal world is consistent, and if so, then it makes sense that if an inmate gets mad at me for being in his cell and yells at me to get out, then a patient in pain can cry out as I walk past their room whether they are sane or not. If spirits can find the energy to threaten humans when we come near, then they can find the energy to moan or scream also.

But that also muddies up the distinction between intelligent and residual hauntings. Can a spirit be classified as intelligent if it is not sane? On the flip side, can it be classified as residual if it is just a spirit who still thinks it is in its hospital bed, mentally ill or not? The spirits at Essex might even be classified as something new—an intelligent spirit who still is not aware of its surroundings and continually cries out in pain over and over again.

Moans are only one part of this group of spirits. There are others who scream out as if trying to get someone's attention or are reliving the last moments of their lives. At the Trans-Allegheny Lunatic Asylum in Weston, West Virginia, I heard the longest and clearest scream of all my experiences. It was six seconds long and so clear that it was captured on both camera audio and a digital recorder.

Screams and crying can be characterized the same way— the emotional outbursts of those who spent their last living moments in agony, guilt, sadness, confusion, or any other turbulent mental state. I encounter these phenomena so often that it leads me to theorize that unstable spirits can't cross over to whatever lies beyond the physical plane. Spirits with emotional baggage or unfinished business are the ones who stick around our world, while those with a clear conscience or who are at peace with their situation go to that great beyond.

I've said it before and I'll say it again—the emotional highs and lows are the hardest part of being a paranormal investigator. Those who think they can just poke around a dark building and walk away unscathed are in for a rude awakening. Contacting the spirit of a deceased person makes you question your own mental well-being and forces you to be a Johnny-on-the-spot psychiatrist. You try to empathize with the subjects and draw them out using objects or people that meant something to them while they were alive and might still. At the end of the day, it's hard to walk away and wash your hands clean of someone who languishes in pain in between worlds and forget about it.

There are so many places that I've been and so many spirits who have had a profound impact on me that taking care of my own mental health becomes a priority at times. But building a wall and separating yourself from the spirits is not the answer. If they sense that you don't care, then they won't either. I think someone who's cold toward these spirits is actually a skeptic because they don't really believe that they're making contact in the first place or they don't care about the subject. They are there to simply capture a piece of evidence and run off with it. I'd rather feel their pain than just my own indifference.

SECTION
IV
Anger

I hate bullies. It's a personal thing, but bullies are next to pond scum on the worthless scale as far as I'm concerned. Just about everyone has experienced confrontation and schoolyard fights growing up. It's what youths do and is pretty much a rite of teenage passage, but getting over it is also a necessary step in the process of maturing. Unfortunately there are some people who never forego their aggressive ways and walk through life daring anyone to knock the chip off their shoulder. Even in death they prey on the weak the same way they did in life.

I've encountered spirits who bully other spirits and take pleasure in intimidating the living. This happens frequently in the dark holes that we toss the worst of humanity into, like prisons, penitentiaries, and reformatories, where the meanest of the mean spent their days. Often emotionally unstable, we sequester them with their own kind behind mammoth stone walls so we don't have to gaze upon life's castaways and only think about them when a Johnny Cash song catches our ear. We do this for the public good, but also because seeing them reminds us of our own fallibility.

I've investigated a lot of places where disturbed people once lived and died, but at the Amargosa Opera House and Hotel in Death Valley Junction, California, I encountered a spirit who made Caligula seem like a saint. The employees of the hotel called him The Boss Man and our fixer (a local paranormal investigator) said he liked to taunt people, push them, feel them, scratch them, and do generally malevolent things, even to the hotel staff. He was the type to raise up to a challenge—the bigger and more aggressive the human, the more active he was. Some people would scare away from this, but I go in the opposite direction and get excited for a confrontation. He's nothing more than a bully and has to be dealt with accordingly.

"Take my energy. I welcome it," I told him during the daytime walkthrough. I needed to coax him out, a tactic that agitated our fixer and made her concerned for my well-being. I didn't care though. If everyone continues to take a soft approach to spirits like The Boss Man, then they just continue to torment the living. I can't stomach that, and I set about taking the fight to him instead of waiting for him to come to me. It's risky of course, but in death as in life, being a victim gets you nowhere. Every year thousands of people have violent paranormal experiences with aggressive spirits and walk away from it scared or confused. They need to know they're not alone and that someone is on their side. I was eager to confront The Boss Man, but I would have to wait several long hours until the sun went down and the conditions were right. Hold that thought.

The Signs of Omens

Sunset is the time between what you know and what you don't. For paranormal investigators it's the moment before you step into the cage. Neither adversary is injured. There's been no contact, no engagement, and no pain. There's only hope, fear, expectations, and a whole lot of unknown that challenges you to understand it. I'd like to say it's the quiet before the storm, but for me it's always a busy time when I'm getting the last few cameras set up or going over the game plan one last time. Yet even when I'm surrounded by technology and people, omens seem to happen.

In Boise, Idaho, I was an hour away from conducting an investigation of the Old Idaho State Prison when black storm clouds blew in from the west and the temperature suddenly dropped. That wasn't significant by itself, but two gaping holes in the sky opened up over the prison like eyes looking down on us. It was a meteorological phenomenon, but it still gave me a feeling that something memorable was going to happen during the night. On that investigation we caught an apparition on film during an instrumental transcommunication session that I believe was the spirit of Raymond Snowden, a murderer who was executed by hanging just feet from where our equipment was at the time.

In Italy I was in a boat heading to Poveglia Island when an X formed by the contrails of two airplanes appeared in the skies over the island just as the sun was setting. That night proved to be one of the most active and violent investigations I've ever conducted. I experienced a near-possession and felt a rage like no other course through my body as the tormented souls of Poveglia made contact with me.

On the day that I was supposed to investigate the abandoned Vulture Mine in Maricopa County, Arizona, a flash flood tore through the only road in and completely blocked it. There was more rain in three hours than in all of 2009 for that area, on the same night as our lockdown. So we were forced to wait until the following evening to conduct our investigation.

The morning after my first investigation of Bobby Mackey's Music World, probably the most evil location in the world, I learned how close my crew and I came to death. A landslide had crashed down the hill outside the building during the night, which we never heard. Had that landslide been twenty feet closer, it could have taken the building off its foundation and swept it into the Licking River with us in it.

In Sacramento, the city flooded. In Chattanooga I nearly missed being crushed by a dock that lifted off its foundation and flipped during a freak storm. Some will say these incidents are pure coincidence, but I've been around the paranormal long enough to feel otherwise. I see the signs around me now. I believe in serendipity, fate, and karma, though not enough to say we don't all have our own free will. The signs that I encountered were at some of the most heinous places I've investigated, and looking back on Bobby Mackey's, I think the experiences we had there were warnings. The entities living there didn't like us and didn't want us to come back.

Too bad I don't listen.

Stirring Up Trouble

I'm a different person when I investigate. I'm not a mouthy guy by nature, but when I get in the midst of evil or hurtful entities, I become the arrogant guy at a party who looks the linebacker in the eye and challenges him and the entire defensive line to a duel. I taunt and provoke, but you have to understand that I do that for a reason. I want to elicit a response. Remember that my mission is to capture on film and digital recording devices evidence of the paranormal. Many times, I can't do that by being nice.

The spirits that roam places where humans were incarcerated only respect strength and courage. They're like Mixed Martial Arts fighters. In their world everyone is tough. What sets one tough guy apart from every other tough guy is respect. So I don't come into a place where dangerous men lived (and killed) each other with a plate of cornbread and cookies. I come in there with the attitude of a Barn Boss wanting to get a response or it's a waste of time. In prison you can't be a victim (not that I know personally).

I only provoke nasty spirits. When I investigate a building with a reported child haunting it, I take a different approach. Scaring a child or even a well-intentioned spirit of an adult will only cause them to retreat and hide, and that gets you nowhere. Provocation is a form of emotional investigation. The goal is to appeal to the spirits emotions, either good or bad, to get them to manifest by either sight or sound. Other investigators have their own style, such as scientific investigation that only seeks data and sensitivity investigation that places emphasis on using mediums, parapsychologists, and sensitives to make contact. I feel each form has its strengths and I try to take the best parts of each one and use them to my advantage. Prisons make developing a plan of attack easy.

Every man either fears prison or has the same morbid curiosity about it as rubberneckers on the highway that pass an accident and slow down to catch a glimpse of a corpse. I'm both. I watch shows like *Lockdown* and *Gangland* and try to imagine how miserable it would be to get caught up in that world, and at the same time thank God I've never had to know. The thought of an oppressed life with little to no hope scares me to the core. Ohio State Reformatory is one such place.

Located between Columbus and Cleveland in the center of America's heartland, OSR had over 155,000 inmates during its 104-year history from 1886 to 1990. Two hundred deaths took place behind its giant walls and eerie Romanesque architecture, which was meant to encourage inmates back to a "rebirth" of their spiritual lives. The architecture was designed to inspire convicts to turn away from their sinful lifestyle and toward repentance. These techniques were abandoned when it became clear they didn't work. Now the prison makes a perfect backdrop for Hollywood films, including *The Shawshank Redemption*.

Almost immediately we had power drains on our equipment, and to be honest, it made me angry. "Are you stealing some energy for the fight tonight?" I yelled out, hoping a challenge would entice the dark spirits out. Former serial killers and violent offenders were attacking people every day, and showing weakness was just going to make me another notch in their belt. Not happening. "You may startle us, but we will not run from you! Your attacks are going to stop!"

I got into character. I grabbed a Billy club and a set of keys and walked down the rows of musty old cells, telling the inmates, "I'm the new guard here." I rapped the club on the bars and got arrogant. In some investigations a soft "good cop" approach is the best way to get a response, but not here. Good cops get nowhere. Bad cops get results.

For those of us who have never been incarcerated, you would think a prison is a prison, but even among hardened criminals there's a hierarchy of fear when it comes to penal institutions. Experienced convicts have a list of prisons that they do and don't want to be sentenced to, and Moundsville Penitentiary in Moundsville, West Virginia, topped the list of don'ts. Over its 119-year history, few other prisons were as bloody or violent. Almost one thousand men are confirmed to have died behind the walls of Moundsville, giving it the dubious distinction of being one of the Department of Justice's top ten most violent correctional facilities ever. Its reputation was well earned, and not just for the harsh living conditions. The unbridled rage spilled over during several riots within its walls, in which both prisoners and guards perished.

Getting locked into Moundsville after dark was not as much fun as I thought it would be. Walking through the prison with Red Bone, whom we never expected to meet, and hearing his stories of the atrocities that happened there amped me up, and I will admit . . . I was a little scared. I was in the middle of a maximum security penitentiary where some of the most hardened criminals in the country had been stored away for safe keeping. It's hard to keep those emotions bottled up and focus on making contact with the spirits who were there. Fear, apprehension, and nerves can influence an investigator and make the rustling of leaves sound like a human voice, so I had to force myself to keep cool and focus. Eventually I found the moral courage to say, "Game on. Let's do this!" I felt like a warrior going to battle with evil entities who wanted to do people harm. Put a symbol on my chest and call me Count Zakula—The Banisher of Evil.

In the bowels of the prison I was alone in the boiler room where they found inmate R. D. Wall's head (he was decapitated during a riot while using the bathroom) and a lot of other negative things happened. This is where Aaron and I heard intelligent responses, which we thought were from R. D. Wall. Then the temperature dropped and our breath became visible, so I decided it was time to be alone. I told Nick and Aaron to go upstairs, and I remained where I was. As I said, it's not easy to put away your own emotions in such a desolate place, especially when you're alone. But when I started getting my evidence, that's when things changed. It was no longer an empty building where bad stuff happened. It was now occupied. It had residents who didn't want me to be there. That in itself was enough to refocus me and—to be honest—make me angry.

"There's a new guard in here and I'm telling you to get back in your cells!" I demanded while in one of the prison wings. "Get your heads up against those bars!" I added for good measure while rolling on my digital recorder. I was hoping I could anger the spirit of a former inmate and get him to react. It did.

Electronic Voice Phenomena

"I'll kill you," the angry spirit responded. It wasn't just what he said, but how he said it. I could hear the rage in his words and the sincerity of his threat. I had invaded his space, challenged his superiority over the cell block, and taunted his manhood. So he replied the only way he could—by threatening me.

The voice was captured on my digital recorder. Deciphering EVPs accurately is an art. What we didn't realize until after the Moundsville investigation was that there was an EVP within the EVP. When we put the recording on the waveform software with EVP experts Mark and Debbie Constantino, we saw that there was a voice within the voice. We only thought it said, "I'll kill you," but in fact there was more. It actually said, "Look up, I've gone away. Look, I'll kill you." At the time I was by myself, so looking back on it, I feel like the spirit was playing with me. That's something a prisoner would have done.

Usually an EVP has a time lag since you have to rewind the recorder and listen to the result, though advances in technology by people like Gary Galka have made it possible to hear EVPs as they happen in real time. It's this lag in time that makes EVP procedures very important.

You would think an EVP captured on two different recorders at the same time would be great evidence, and in fact that happens occasionally, but overall it's very rare. A voice on two recorders is usually not a disembodied voice, but a human voice that came from somewhere close or was spoken by a living person in the room.

I'm very strict when it comes to EVP sessions. You have to be very cautious and take it very seriously when you hit record on that digital recorder because the last thing you want is to hear feet shuffling or your friends whispering and mistake them for spirits when you review your data. Here are my rules for a successful EVP session:

1. Identify a leader in the session and make sure that leader takes charge of the session.
2. Do burst EVP sessions—about one to two minutes each.
3. Ask five or six leading questions so you can increase your chances of getting more than one intelligent response.
4. Ensure everyone remains still and quiet for the duration of the session to reduce the possibility of noise contamination. Eliminate all forms of noise that could later lead to auditory paredolia (incorrectly interpreting random noises as familiar patterns).
5. If something happens during the session that could be later confused for a spirit noise, call it out.

6. If someone hears or feels a presence during the session, identify it by speaking up.
7. Review the recordings on the spot so you know that if you got something it happened right there and then. That way it's fresh in everyone's minds and you can hopefully get a feel for the emotional state of the entity for the rest of your investigation.

A way to avoid criticism when you capture an EVP is to analyze it on a computer using audio editing software. I always do this to examine the waveform and wavelengths. After doing this for a few years now, I've noticed an emerging pattern. With almost every EVP, there is an associated blip in the waveform that we call a frequency pop. It's a small spike that precedes the disembodied voice that I feel is an additional indicator of the presence of a spirit. This frequency pop is similar to the sonic boom an aircraft creates when it passes through the sound barrier.

When it comes to EVPs, paranormal investigators like Billy Tolley of Las Vegas Paranormal Investigations of Mysterious Phenomena (Las Vegas PIMPs—catchy) are like cardiologists looking at an electrocardiogram. They've learned to sift through the noise and focus on what's important and relevant to the ghost hunter. They can distinguish a disembodied voice from a cough, which makes having one at your disposal invaluable.

All paranormal investigators have an EVP that they hold dear to them like Gollum holds on to his precious ring. For many of us, it's that one piece of evidence that either justifies what we do, validates our belief in the paranormal, or was a life-changing personal experience. For me, one EVP captured at the Goldfield Hotel in Nevada when I was still an inexperienced investigator really opened my eyes not only to the realities of EVP, but to the possibility that some spirits remember the impact we had on them just as much as we remember the impact they had on us.

Nevada is full of haunted locations. A volatile combination of corporate greed, prospector hope, and untimely violent death permeate the state's barren terrain and treeless, yet stunning landscapes. The town of Goldfield, just south of Reno, was subject to the same get-rich-quick-or-die-trying fever as almost every other Nevada town with a mine in the nineteenth century. It was the definition of a boomtown, exploding from nothing to 35,000 people between 1902 and 1904. But eight short years later, the ore began running out and the people started running away. By 1920, the gold was almost gone and the town was reduced to just about 1,500 people. Three years later, a devastating fire wiped out twenty-seven blocks of homes and businesses.

In 1908, at the height of its popularity, the Goldfield Hotel was built on the former site of the Nevada Hotel, which had burned down in 1905. It was a grand spectacle with four stories of stone and brick and 154 rooms loaded with the latest technology—telephones, electric lights, and heated steam. The lobby was paneled with mahogany and furnished in black leather upholstery beneath gold-leaf ceilings and crystal chandeliers. The Goldfield Hotel imported chefs from Europe and boasted one of the first Otis elevators west of the Mississippi River. In the middle of nowhere, this hotel was considered the most luxurious between Chicago and San Francisco. It appealed to society's upper crust, making it an immediate success.

George Wingfield, primary owner of the Goldfield Consolidated Mines Company, bought the hotel a short time after it was built. Wingfield was a multimillionaire by the age of thirty and became a political powerhouse in the state of Nevada, running both the Republican and Democratic parties as well as twelve banks. So it was an embarrassing situation for him when a prostitute named Elizabeth turned up pregnant, claiming the child was his. Fearful of how this scandal might affect his business affairs, Wingfield allegedly lured Elizabeth to room 109 of the hotel and chained her to a radiator. Reportedly she cried out over and over for mercy, but found none. Some say that Elizabeth died in childbirth, but others contend that Wingfield murdered her after the child was born and he had tossed the baby down an old mining shaft under the hotel. Rumors abound that Elizabeth haunts the hotel and the sound of a crying child can be heard coming from the basement.

With only five hundred permanent residents, none of whom seem to come out in the daylight, it feels like the town in *The Hills Have Eyes*. I first visited the town in 2004 when we made our documentary film and captured the infamous flying brick incident; still one of the seminal moments of my life. The short version of the story goes like this—while investigating the basement of the Goldfield Hotel, a brick lifted off the ground and flew at Aaron and me. At the same time, an old piece of wood behind the brick danced in the air and turned in strange circles that could only be described as influenced by something other than the forces of gravity. We had that footage validated by professional video analyst Slim Ritchie and PhD Victor Kwong of the UNLV physics department to prove it was no hoax. It was an incredible moment that I still consider the best piece of paranormal phenomena caught on film and one of the scariest moments of my life.

Now here's the story you didn't hear. After our documentary aired, paranormal investigators Mark and Debbie Constantino went into the Goldfield Hotel with Reno reporter Bill Brown, a skeptic. During multiple EVP sessions they'd gotten no responses, so with the night ending they decided to split up in the basement of the hotel. Then something happened that took the evening in a whole new direction.

With her digital recorder rolling, Debbie asked a question. "Tell us what you want us to know."

"Get ready to believe," a voice responded. Debbie then asked about the flying brick incident.

"There are people here saying that you did this. Did you actually do it?" The response blew them all away. A voice, whose clarity is unmatched in digital recordings replied, "Thank you, but we've done it."

It was an intelligent response to a deliberate question and the clarity of the recording was impeccable. This wasn't a static-laden recording that you have to struggle to make out. It was clear, vocal conversation, captured at a frequency well above the normal range of human speech.

As for Bill, he would later admit, "I know what I felt, saw, and heard. I'm not sure who or what it was, but I know something, someone was there and it wasn't always nice." That one piece of evidence changed his outlook, which is a testament to the power of EVPs.

I really feel that the Constantino's and myself have pushed the boundaries of EVP over the last few years and helped advanced communications between the realms. I once captured an EVP of a spirit that said, "Can I ask a question?" That incident validated that we're making strides toward helping humans communicate with spirits and vice versa. While there is no formal classification system of EVPs that is accepted across the paranormal research field, a few groups have developed an informal classification system. Here's how I define the different types of EVPs:

Class A—The recording has a full tone and clear message that needs no enhancement the first time you hear it. This is usually an intelligent response to a deliberate question. The recording of Jonathon Widders at Houghton Mansion is a great example of a Class A EVP.

Class B—The recording has little tone and may or may not have intelligence associated with it. The investigator has to listen closely and repeatedly to decipher the message. Clarity is not as good as Class A. Clear screams, growls, singing, groans, and humming are good examples.

Class C—The recording resembles a harsh whisper and takes time to decipher. External equipment is required to fully recognize the message and sometimes there may be only syllables with no clear words.

Class D—Poor quality recording and questionable if it's even an EVP. An unexplained voice with undecipherable words or noises.

Splitting Up

Humans take comfort in numbers. We feel more secure in a group environment and get jittery when alone, especially in a place like Hillview Manor, where there are miles and miles of tunnels. But it's a necessary step in the paranormal investigation process. Splitting up allows us to cover more ground, but it has other benefits as well. When we're together we sometimes miss EVP recordings because we're talking or focusing our cameras on each other instead of at the environment. So I always spend time alone and have Nick and Aaron do the same to tune ourselves in to the environment, but more importantly because some spirits don't want to approach us as a group.

Keep in mind that many spirits don't know they're dead and are confused by the presence of three guys with cameras invading their space. They can feel intimidated, afraid, or even angry and retreat to someplace comfortable in the cracks of the building to not be seen. By splitting up and going into different parts of the location alone, we make the relationship more personal and get better results. Of course being alone also cranks the fear dial up a few thousand notches and makes self-discipline more important than ever. Controlling your emotions on an investigation isn't so tough when your friends are around to comfort you, but alone in the dark, your only companions are your courage and character. It's where amateurs panic. I love it.

Apparitions

Nevada has always been one of my favorite places to investigate because the history and landscape of the state are full of crushed hopes and dashed dreams. Tales abound of hearty men braving the journey from all parts to come here prospecting for a better future, few of which ended in success. The rough and tumble mining towns arguably saw more tragedy and heartbreak than any other part of the country other than the bloody Civil War battlefields of the East Coast.

While filming my documentary in 2004 we captured a full-bodied apparition as it walked across the top floor of the Old Washoe Club in Virginia City, Nevada, just behind my partner, Nick Groff. It was a man, who walked from left to right across the camera and was one of the clearest apparitions ever caught on film.

Old Washoe Club.

Apparitions have the most emotional impact on the observer and frequently make believers out of skeptics, yet I had to defend my piece of evidence repeatedly to the naysayers. Part of the public's disbelief stems from their own personal values (mostly family and religion), but a lot of skepticism comes from the advances in technology that make film editing easy, even for the amateur home video enthusiast. That's understandable, so I went to great lengths to debunk the Old Washoe Club footage, taking it once again to video professional Slim Ritchie to prove that the film had not been tampered with. Under the scrutiny of an oscilloscope, he verified that it was genuine (Film critic Josh Bell of *Las Vegas Weekly* magazine would later call this piece of evidence, "the most convincing of the supernatural.")

Apparitions are the hardest to capture by modern technology. We're constantly trying new ways to capture apparitions, like full spectrum cameras, infrared, and ultraviolet. I don't think we'll ever find a spectrum of light that makes our world like the movie *Thirteen Ghosts*, where the characters had special glasses they wore that illuminated all the spirits around them. When the conditions are right and an apparition is visible, it's like a lightning storm in the desert—it's rare, but it happens, and when it does, it's quick.

Apparitions are the Holy Grail of paranormal investigation because they're rarely caught on film and even when they are, the paranormal investigator faces an uphill battle to get people to believe the evidence. Everyone has a gold standard of their profession—scoring a touchdown, landing a big client, getting a Christmas bonus. It's the main goal of what you do. For me, capturing an apparition on film is the pinnacle of achievement.

Apparitions are not the same as ectoplasm mists. They usually appear in a complete human form instead of being just an odd, moving shape with no outline. One of the strangest things about apparitions is that they are frequently observed wearing clothes, usually the clothes they wore while alive. Apparitions have been seen in period garb from flowing, nineteenth–century, *"Gone with the Wind"* dresses to modern-day bikinis and everything in between. It's one of the great mysteries of the paranormal: Why do people take their clothes with them after death? An apparition I encountered at Sloss Furnace in Birmingham, Alabama, might shed some light on the subject.

It's hard to imagine the most powerful nation on Earth being a broken, dysfunctional remnant of an insane dream called Freedom, but that was the situation in 1865 when the Civil War finally ended. The South was in ruins having endured several invasions from Sherman's scorched-earth march across Georgia to Grant's capture of Vicksburg and the multitudes of battles that ripped Virginia to shreds. Reconstruction was the problem, and iron was the answer. Confederate Colonel James Sloss returned to his native Alabama after years of fighting and helped found the city of Birmingham from three smaller towns. Birmingham quickly found its post-Civil War identity in iron, steel, and railroading, earning the nickname "Pittsburgh of the South." In 1882, Sloss started his own pig-iron-producing plant outside the city that was immediately successful, though Sloss himself got out of the business just four years later.

For eighty-nine years the Sloss Furnace labored night and day, churning out what would become the spine of America— steel. But in 1971, after suffering from years of low iron ore production in Alabama and needing extensive modifications due to the Clean Air Act, Sloss Furnace was closed and the land was donated to the Alabama State Fair Authority to be made into a museum.

Walking through the dilapidated furnace grounds is deceiving. The kid in me sees the intertwined vents and latticed piping as a jungle gym just waiting to be explored like a new play-ground. But the mature adult looks back in time to envision the brutal working conditions and stifling humidity of central Ala-bama and sees nothing but hardship. Add to that the thousand-degree heat of the blast furnaces and the close proximity the men worked to very heavy machinery and it's easy to see why so many of Sloss's employees perished on the job. Men were incinerated, sucked into rotating gears, and fell to their deaths from the furnace's tower all too frequently.

"My daddy used to have a saying," former employee Pat-rick Shelby told me during our walkthrough. "Kill a man, hire another one. Kill a mule buy another one. Don't kill a mule, they cost twenty-five dollars."

I'm glad I don't work in a place where an ass is valuable and a human life is worthless.

We didn't even have a chance to get fully set up before para-normal activity, as unpredictable as ever, started. The sun had just set over the heart of the South and the smell of rusted steel and corroded history hung in the damp air. We didn't have our cameras on and I was trying to determine the best locations to set up static cameras when I looked down a passageway and jumped back at what I saw. A worker, dressed in a white T-shirt and blue denim overalls that reminded me of a 1950s train en-gineer walked from my left to right about thirty feet away from me. He was as visible as any real human that I've ever had a conversation with as he passed into my view and then out of sight through a little opening in the factory's jumble of pipes.

All the air in my body ran away in fright, and I stood there, motionless, trying to comprehend the shockwave rolling through me. It took a moment for my brain to realize that I was indeed a paranormal investigator and my job was to go places most people won't. Letting the moment pass me by would be ir-

Sloss furnace.

responsible, so I willed my legs to move and ran toward the last point that I saw him while calling for Nick and Aaron. When I got there, he was gone and there was no evidence of any human being in the area.

Aaron and Nick did exactly what they were supposed to. They grabbed a camera, asked what I saw, inspected the area themselves, and looked for anything that could debunk it. We looked for any reflective surfaces or possibility of light fooling us and ran in each direction to make sure there was no one in the compound but us. There wasn't.

People who have a long relationship with Sloss Furnace tell a common story of Slag: a sadistic and oppressive foreman. Slag was a generally angry man, taking his frustrations in life out on his employees and making an already difficult job almost unbearable. Finally they enacted revenge on him (allegedly) by pushing him into a large vat of molten steel from behind. I believe that spirits who died suddenly and don't know they're dead go about their business in the same manner as if they were alive. They continue to work as if nothing had changed, and that's why I saw Slag walking the floor of the furnace that evening still dressed in his work clothes. It would stand to reason that a man so used to being in control of his environment would want to still be in control after death and continue doing what he loved to do—work his employees to death.

One theory that attempts to explain apparitions like this is that Slag's energy left an imprint on the universe the same way a foot leaves an imprint in the sand. As we go through our lives our energies leave an imprint on the very fabric that the universe is made of. Just like our hands leave an imprint on a window, our bodily energy leaves a mark on the field, so as Slag walked around the furnace, he left an imprint. And as our energies increase during times of extreme emotion, the imprint gets more pronounced.

Imprint Theory states that everything in the universe is stored on a repository field the same way a computer chip stores data. This field is the very fabric of the universe and everything, including you and I, make an imprint of our energy on that field, especially during times of extreme emotion. I can understand how the living and the spirits (who are also made of energy) can leave a signature behind for us to see under certain conditions, so Imprint Theory to me seems feasible.

But imprint theory is limited. It only explains passive apparitions who are going about their lives as they remember them, and as I described in an earlier chapter, there are definitely intelligent spirits who interact with the living. They maintain their identity after death. Another level of spirit is the mischievous ones, who not only thrive in the afterlife but have a mission as well.

Malevolent Mischief

The untrained or the uneducated try to categorize spirits as either good or bad, black or white, but as with just about everything there are shades of gray. Some entities exist whose intentions are not virtuous, but not purely evil either. These entities seem to have a mission. Overall their goal is harmful to humans, although their ability to actually cause any harm is limited. I've had personal experiences with two.

A poltergeist is not a demon that infects your children through static on your TV set, nor is it something that possesses young girls and makes their heads spin around. I loved the movie, but I'm not drinking that Kool-Aid. Poltergeists are like ghosts on steroids. They're more powerful than normal spirits and have the ability to move objects and transfer their emotions onto the nearest human. They're generally blamed for unexplained noises, missing items, and grumpiness, but they're not as dangerous as most people think. They're capable of pushing people over and even starting small fires, but instances of human injury is rare. If anything, it's their ability to scare that can lead to injury in the cases of people fleeing in panic and running into something.

I believe poltergeists are intelligent entities, but I don't think they're all angry spirits. At the Villisca Axe Murder House in Southwest Iowa, a poltergeist made his presence known by slamming a door very hard that was captured perfectly on a video camera. No one was in the house at the time, so it can't be said this action was aimed at anyone. Instead it seemed like an attention-getting maneuver. There was a clear sound of footsteps approaching and seconds later the door violently slammed shut. There was no wind and no natural slant to the door that would make it close on its own. When it happened it sent a shockwave of energy through the house that we could feel all the way in the barn next door.

I think poltergeists are trying to tell the living something and have more energy to do it, but their way of making contact is sometimes perceived as evil or mischievous. To me, poltergeists are at the top of the spiritual food chain that can be separated by levels of energy and activity. I believe spirits can be classified by their "energy rating."

- Level 1 are weak spirits who pass through you. They reach out and use touch to try to contact the living, resulting in emotions, cold drafts, and goose bumps.

- Level 2 are spirits who communicate through electronic communications such as EVP. This is the most common type of spirit paranormal investigators encounter.

- Level 3 are spirits who manifest visually, like Slag the Foreman. They've either learned to make themselves seen or are residual hauntings.

- Level 4 are spirits who can move objects at will if the conditions are right. These are poltergeists like the one at the Villisca Axe Murder House.

It takes a lot of energy to make an object move, which is why you don't hear a lot about poltergeist activity. Graduating to that level takes time and probably some outside help, making poltergeists a rare find. So why do you have a poltergeist in one building, but across the street there are seventeen weaker spirits? Why do some of these ghosts have the ability to move stuff while others can only muster a voice or a cold chill? Power drains might hold the answer. Poltergeist activity is frequently preceded by local power drains. They need energy from humans, batteries, or equipment to move objects, so when your freshly charged batteries suddenly go straight down to zero, it might be creepy time.

So why do they move stuff around more than other ghosts? Because they can. Imagine if you died and thought you were going to heaven or hell but got stuck here. It can be maddening or even boring, like *Groundhog Day*. Some poltergeists try to harm or scare people because that's their entertainment. If you had the ability to walk among the living and not be detected, but could mess with them, would you? Some people would, some wouldn't. In that sense, poltergeists could be spirits who have learned to use available energy, but are too irresponsible to handle that power.

I think if all ghosts could be poltergeists they would. I firmly believe the spirit world is as it was portrayed in the movie *Ghost*. In that movie there's a scene where Patrick Swayze tried and tried to kick a can but couldn't because he didn't have a body and didn't know how to channel his energy to make it move. Then an experienced ghost shows him how to channel his energy and make the can move with his mind instead of his body.

The convergence of ley lines may have something to do with it. The Goldfield Hotel and the Ancient Ram Inn are built on top of ley line convergences and both have mischievous spirits residing inside. It's possible that the underlying geomagnetic energy of the ley line increases their ability to draw energy and manifest to the point that they can move stuff around.

Ley Lines

Ley lines are the lines drawn on a map between places of geographical interest, such as Stonehenge and Westminster Abbey. The concept of ley lines were first introduced in 1921 by archaeologist Alfred Watkins in his book, *The Old Straight Track*. Watkins theorized that these lines were natural flows of spiritual energy that humans instinctively followed and built monuments and dwellings on top of. Just like birds follow the magnetic field of the Earth when they migrate, humans use these invisible geomagnetic lines to guide us to the most crucial item we need to survive—water.

Ley lines were expanded upon by the British Society of Dowsers when they saw the potential for them to predict the flows of underground rivers and aquastats. It has been theorized that the intersections of ley lines may be points on the Earth where spiritual or psychic energy is enhanced. I'm a believer in ley lines and the flow of geomagnetic fields. I believe that where ley lines intersect there is a vortex of spiritual energy that ghosts can use to manifest.

Few places in the world can boast as much paranormal weirdness as the Ancient Ram Inn in Gloucestershire, England. Built in the twelfth century on top of a five-thousand-year-old pagan burial ground, the Ancient Ram Inn is the oldest building in its area and has a distinguished list of at least fourteen named spirits that still reside there. The building has witnessed countless murders and ritual sacrifices since before recorded history, making it one of the world's most haunted places.

We know the Ancient Ram Inn has been around since

1145—almost as long as William the Conqueror and modern England itself—and may have been built before that. The Inn has been a church house for an unknown period, a Mason's lodge, a slave's quarters, a brewery, and possibly an orphanage. Historic maps suggest the original building could have been three times as large as today's structure, begging the question, "what happened to the other two-thirds?"

The building is something straight out of Harry Potter's Daigon Alley: a mishmash of added-on rooms in different architectural styles from different centuries with no clear reason. Walls lean like they'll fall over at any moment and multicolored bricks make the exterior look like a checkerboard of construction. A tunnel from the back of the main fireplace burrows down into the Earth and emerges at the nearby Saint Mary's Church, and another leads to the Lacock Abbey, most likely for smugglers, which adds to its dubious history. The inn has had eight reported possessions, lies squarely on the intersection of two perpendicular ley lines (just like the Goldfield Hotel), and has verifiable evidence that it was once the site of devil worshipping and the ritual sacrifice of children, making it an irresistible den of spookiness.

The building's caretaker only adds to the weird ambience. When I first met John Humphries, I felt like the Scooby Doo Crew when they rip the mask off the villain and reveal someone they met earlier in the episode. It was such a strange place that I wasn't really surprised when I stepped inside and the putrid odor of an antique store greeted my nose and lungs. It was beyond mere must and funk. It reeked.

As if all that was not enough, the Ancient Ram Inn held a spirit that I had never before or since encountered. It's called a succubus, and according to the legend, it is a female demon that takes the form of a human woman in order to seduce men, usually through sex. It's not as cool as it sounds. It's believed that the succubus steals the life force of the human male in order to regenerate herself. The male version is the incubus (not the band) and it's said that repeated intercourse with either can result in deterioration of health.

"Old Man Humphries" thoroughly believed that the Ancient Ram Inn was haunted by a succubus who could only stay alive through intercourse with him. To protect himself he wore condoms at night, and used wrappers littered the Inn. He wore them at night to keep the succubus from taking his semen. I knew I was going to have to face this spirit, although I was secretly apprehensive. The last thing I wanted was to get an involuntary erection on camera.

Opening a Portal

At the Ancient Ram Inn, I decided to lure the succubus out with an old pagan ritual. Spirits need an opportunity to be seen and heard, so it's the responsibility of the paranormal investigator to create the conditions for that to happen. Spirits, no matter how emotional or disturbed, sometimes need the living to open a portal for them to step through, so I like to experiment with local rituals and untested technology to give them the best chance at making their presence known. Sometimes it works, sometimes it doesn't, and there's always the possibility that you'll open a door for an undesirable spirit (and no, I don't recommend Ouija boards).

Paganism goes back thousands of years in this area, and the Inn itself is believed to be on top of a pagan burial ground where children were ritually sacrificed to their Gods. On one end of the Inn an altar adorned with a goat's head stood in front of a massive stone gothic hearth, so we took advantage of it and enlisted the help of local pagan witch called "Lady Snake."

She brought us into a circle and called upon her deities. "I call on the element of air," she said holding a dagger into the air. "I call upon the elemental of sylph. Please come in to our ritual tonight. I call upon the element of fire and the elemental of salamander." This might seem ridiculous, but when you're trying to find answers to some of life's most elusive questions, it's necessary to try anything.

To be honest, I was hesitant because I was getting a bad feeling about this place and this ritual. When Lady Snake informed us that she could no longer continue because she feared for her own life, I seriously considered calling it off. I thought we might be going too far.

"I've done a part of the ritual for you that specifically states that you will give a gift," she told us. "And that gift has to be you." She made a case for us already being past the point of no return.

But Aaron wasn't having it and countered with the reasons why we should stop. "You know what follows us home," he said, referring to the spirits that have attached themselves to us and appeared at our own homes.

"So what's one more spirit following us home?" I pointed out.

"The major motherload of all is what," Aaron protested. He was right to be concerned, and in the end it's always good to have a dissenting voice when it comes to something risky like this. He was just looking out for all of us. But we'd come too far to back down. Something was waiting for us to make contact, and no matter how dangerous it was, I was going to see the ritual through.

Lady Snake instructed me to lie down on the floor in front

of the fireplace with my legs spread eagle like a sacrifice. A deep growl arose from the altar as I lay supine on the floor. I had never felt more like bait. I felt the distinct feeling of hands moving up my thighs and my breath suddenly became visible. It had not been cold enough all day for our breath to be visible, and even that night the temperature did not drop low enough to make it happen.

"She's in," Lady Snake said.

"In what?" I responded. At that moment another loud growl came from the altar. What seemed like a laughable skit earlier now turned deadly serious. You can wave this off as impossible, but the reality is that this pagan witch called upon a spirit, offering me as a gift. Something took it.

Lady Snake became fearful and refused to finish the ritual. She asked a goddess for protection and stopped. "In the next few days something will happen to you, and I wish you luck."

I didn't understand the severity of the ritual at the time. After the investigation I had a violent nightmare in my London hotel room. During the dream, a lady with extremely long fingernails was scratching at my face as I tried to fight her off. I woke thinking it was over, but it wasn't. The next morning Aaron noticed something on my neck and when I inspected it, there were three scratches running down the side of it. It was very strange.

The Ancient Ram Inn isn't just any old location out in someone's backyard. This is one of the oldest civilizations known to man and a nearly nine-hundred-year-old building where dark entities have been called upon thousands of times. It was powerful, but in the end it was worth it. That evening we had a lot of paranormal activity at the Inn. We even caught EVPs in British accents (female voices). I don't ascribe all our activity to the ritual, but I think it certainly opened a door for spirits to wander through.

Indigenous ceremonies like this one help me connect to my target entities. It's like Neo plugging in to the matrix, and it hyper-sensitizes me to the environment like a sniper. I'm programming my body, which is my most important piece of equipment, with the culture of the people I'm investigating. I continually modify and improve my body by plugging it into the environment. I don't recommend people do this on their own. This is my life. It's what I do.

I had a similar experience at Magnolia Lane Plantation. I'd never been to Louisiana, so I was anxious to see if all the tall tales of voodoo and witchcraft had any credibility or were just fanciful pseudoscience. Located in the backwaters of central Louisiana, Magnolia Lane Plantation was constructed in the early nineteenth century and became an operating cotton plantation around 1830. For over one hundred years the Plantation grew assorted crops until the majority of its workers migrated away from the countryside to urban cities. Today the expansive estate is a National Park with twenty-one intact buildings, including eight red brick cabins that once housed slaves and tenant farmhands.

The plantation has a bloody past. An overseer was shot and killed in the front yard of the main house during the Civil War and buried where he fell. In the basement of the house, iron leg shackles still sit in the same place they did when slaves were bound for days at a time for punishment.

Many of Magnolia Lane's slaves practiced voodoo and placed curses on the plantation's owners throughout the years. Half of the students of the University of Houston anthropology department refuse to go to the plantation at night because they feel it's just too creepy. That's what I like to hear. If there's a

Three scratches on my neck
received during a violent nightmare
in my London hotel room after luring out
a succubus with an old Pagan ritual
at the Ancient Ram Inn.

place that people are too frightened to venture into, call me.

Like the Ancient Ram Inn, this investigation gave me an opportunity to push the boundaries. I feel you have to identify with the spirits you're after. One of the spirits said to haunt the slave cabins is that of a high voodoo priestess, which made me wonder—if she was in tune with the spirit world when she was alive, would she still be familiar with the boundaries between the two worlds? If she knew how to open the door when she was alive, would she still from the other side?

I decided to indulge in a local voodoo ritual to find out more about this misunderstood culture and hopefully pave the way for active spirit communication the next evening. Under a grove of giant oak trees dripping with Spanish moss, we met with the voodoo queen of Louisiana, Bloody Mary, after the sun went down. It's probably the only time I've worn a white T-shirt and doo-rag, but you do what you have to do when it comes to ghosts.

"Legba," she said while shaking her bells. "He is the gate-keeper between this world and the next. He is the voodoo Jesus. Open the door, Legba." She parted the veil and we all felt a huge wave of energy come through our circle of torches. It hit me first, then Aaron then Nick then Bloody Mary and was with-out a doubt some form of spirit that she had awakened. During the ritual, a member of our crew snapped several photos, one of which held a frightening apparition of a woman's face in the smoke behind a flame. There were distinct eyes, eyebrows, a hairline, and a nose.

I immediately tried to debunk it. I can look at a mirror and find fifty faces in it. I can look at a dirty window and see the im-age of several kids. So I know how the mind matrixes and finds identifiable patterns. But this was different. It wasn't the face of Jesus in a piece of toast. It was a woman and it stared back at the camera, inviting us to learn more about her. The next night we captured a lot of paranormal activity, and I'm convinced Bloody Mary's parting of the veil helped make that happen. When dawn came and our time at Magnolia Lane was over, I took the voodoo doll that Bloody Mary gave me and left it on the floor of one slave cabin as she instructed me to.

But not every door has to be opened through ancient rituals or voodoo magic. Sometimes you can open a door for spiritual communication with modern technology. That's exactly what I did in Idaho State Penitentiary.

Idaho was little more than a lawless territory in 1870 when construction began on a new jail that would eventually witness several deaths inside its sandstone walls, quarried by prisoners from the ridges that surround Boise. Nestled against these barren, brown ridges, the prison became a macabre amphitheater during executions, since they were normally hangings carried out in the open courtyard. Citizens from Boise would come to watch hangings from the elevated heights that offered a perfect view of the proceedings over the walls. Ten people were executed in the Idaho State Penitentiary, including the state's only double-execution hanging.

Determined to avoid making his death a public spectacle, Douglas Van Vlack, a convict sentenced to be executed for kidnapping and murdering his wife and two police officers, took matters into his own hands. The day he was slated to die, Van Vlack escaped his guards, climbed into the rafters of the prison and stayed there contemplating his death. As the guards closed in on him, Van Vlack jumped, smashing into the concrete floor below and dying five hours later.

Like many prisons, Idaho State Pen also had its share of riots. In 1971 and 1973 prisoners, angry at the living conditions inside the walls, rose up in revolt. Several were shot during the 1971 riot while trying to escape. Another was killed by his fellow inmates and rolled up into a gym mat. The 1973 riot also resulted in major damage, and one inmate was gang raped to death.

The Idaho State Penitentiary is a vortex of pent up rage. The facility incorporated the "Pennsylvania System" of reform that emphasized isolation, labor, and religious reflection as a means to seek penitence and remorse from the inmates. Like others that incorporated the system, it was eventually abandoned due to high suicide rates and the increase in mental illness. The residual suffering of the prison is represented by the tale of Idaho's Jack the Ripper, Raymond Allen Snowden. Snowden was convicted of the murder of Cora Dean and sentenced to death by hanging. By some accounts, Snowden hung by his neck for fifteen minutes before he died. He was the first and only prisoner hanged in the new gallows and is the last person executed by hanging in Idaho. It's the spirit of Ray Snowden that I believe I encountered while trying to use technology to open a portal for him to communicate.

Instrumental Transcommunication is not an indigenous ritual (obviously), but it serves the same purpose—it opens a doorway for spirits to communicate. It works by setting up a video camera five feet from a TV, pointed directly at it. The camera is connected directly to the TV so that it shows what the video camera is capturing (the TV). This creates a video feedback loop that allows spirits to make themselves seen. After recording for a set period of time, it's best to analyze the footage on a computer with the right movie editing software, just as we do with EVPs.

The drawback to ITC is that it's time intensive. The video camera shoots at thirty frames per second, so if you shoot ITC for thirty seconds, then you have nine hundred frames to go through one by one to see if you captured anything. If a spirit decides it doesn't want to be seen in those thirty seconds then you've wasted a lot of time. So using ITC is a gamble. Fortunately for us, it paid off.

We conducted ITC in the gallows of Idaho State Penitentiary where Raymond Snowden was executed and caught an image that looks very much like a man with a skinny neck wearing a hooded cloth. The image clearly had a head, neck, and shoulders and was exactly what I was hoping we'd find.

We did three ITC sessions that evening, resulting in 2,700 video frames. Only three frames had this image, so it can't be explained as any sort of repeated pattern or glitch in the video. The image jumped out and stayed for one-tenth of a second, just long enough to see, but not make any real contact. For this image to suddenly appear and then disappear couldn't be explained away as a malfunction of technology or random interference. Like Slag who left his imprint on the floors of Sloss Furnace, this could be the imprint that Raymond Snowden left on the universe just before he died. Just imagine the emotional and pain-induced charged energy as Snowden was hanging for fifteen minutes to die at the end of that rope. I feel that energy manifested itself onto our ITC experiment.

In the same room earlier in the investigation we caught a picture of a black mist hovering over my shoulder. The two pieces of evidence convinced me that we were in the presence of Raymond's spirit. A third data point, like a spike in EMF, an EVP voice, or a drop in temperature would have made this encounter ironclad. Second and third data points boost the credibility of a paranormal experience, and in a different prison I had that very encounter.

Face Your Fears

Fear is a product of knowing the consequences of your actions. If you don't know how badly you can get hurt doing something, then it's easy to be fearless. Small children aren't afraid of much because they don't really understand the concept of getting hurt or killed. Instead of being afraid of flying they just see it as a fun ride because they don't know how a crash can result in maiming and death. If you've never experienced the stinging pain of a broken nose or the nauseating sickness of a kick to the liver, then you might not be afraid to get into a fistfight.

I know what can happen during a paranormal investigation, so I carry some fear around with me, but it's actually the dangers of this physical realm that scare me more. I'm afraid of snakes, open water, and heights. But I also believe you can't let phobias dictate how you live your life, so I face my fears whenever I can to get over them.

At Castillo de San Marcos I rowed a little canoe across an open channel with a current so strong that the Rescue Officer made us aware how easy we could drown if we toppled over and he wouldn't be able to rescue us. I love Aaron Goodwin like a brother, but he's also the Will Ferrell of paranormal investigation. He's big and clumsy, which rocked the canoe and took my fears up to 11.

At Idaho State Penitentiary I handled a wild snake. At Sloss Furnace, I climbed the massive rusty, eroding water tower with missing bolts on every stair to get a clear view of the grounds and try to experience what the men who worked there did. Many men fell to their deaths from this tower, and combined with my acrophobia, my legs wobbled more and more with every passing stair.

By the time I got to the top, I was gripping anything solid with every muscle I had, convinced the whole thing would topple over at any moment (hey, the dudes who were there even said we were crazy to climb it). It wasn't a publicity stunt or a dramatic effect for the show. It was a real fear that I felt needed to be attacked head-on to grow as a person, although all I could think of was, "How high are we?" I've never kissed the ground before, but Alabama soil nearly got a big smooch when I got back down.

Temperature Fluctuations

An old paranormal theory is that manifesting spirits cause the ambient temperature to drop or even rise. If we assume spirits are made of weak energy and have to absorb more energy to manifest into an apparition or a disembodied voice, then it's plausible to theorize that they absorb heat when they manifest as well. This can cause the temperature to drop in the immediate vicinity of the spirit.

There's a theory that spirits cause temperature drops because as they absorb energy in the room. They cause the ambient temperature to decrease the same way rain droplets absorb heat as they pass through the air (ever stand on a porch and feel fine, but then step out into the rain and feel really cold?).

I was investigating a room at Moundsville State Penitentiary with one camera in my hand and a static night vision camera in one corner so it could record any external changes in the environment. Until this point in the night, the temperature had been relatively comfortable. It was cool, but not cold. At the exact same moment that I captured an EVP, my breath suddenly became visible when I exhaled. When you see your breath, you are seeing water droplets condense. The air has to be cool to do this, but there's no set temperature for it to happen because it also depends on what the air pressure is at the time. All night I had only seen my breath once—when Aaron and I felt a presence on the main level of the prison. Now here it was again at the same time a spirit threatened me in an EVP.

Coldness, though, is not a piece of evidence by itself unless you're in the middle of Arkansas in summer and a thermometer suddenly drops to forty degrees. Buildings exhibit natural temperature variances and pockets of cold air move freely. Also most paranormal investigations take place just after sunset, when the temperature begins to drop until sunrise starts to bring it back up again. However, a sudden drop in temperature in conjunction with an EVP adds a second data point and legitimacy to the evidence.

There are two main types of thermometers for paranormal investigators—regular thermometers that measure ambient air temperature in its immediate area and infrared thermometers that measure surface temperature from a distance. Infrared thermometers are useful because they let you read a temperature from several feet away, so when you hear a noise or think you see an apparition you can take a temperature reading quickly without running toward it and scaring it away.

Some spirits run from humans. Some don't.

The Dangers of Paranormal Investigation

I once had a fan write to say thank you for showing him that there's nothing to be afraid of when it comes to ghosts. He was afflicted by a paralyzing fear of the paranormal and refused to watch any movies or TV shows that even had a hint of the afterlife in it, never mind a horror flick. Despite that, one day he decided to face his fears and watch *Ghost Adventures* (though he says it was from behind a couch and he couldn't sleep that night). Still he kept with it and ended up watching every show. When he realized that no real physical harm came to any of us, he got over his fear of the paranormal and is now an investigator in the Washington, D.C., area.

I think that's a great story, but there's a big difference between the average residential haunting and the dark demons I encounter. There's a balance to be struck between the simple investigation that consists of nothing more than a few EVPs and the evil entities I've run across that stay with me. Keep in mind that what you see on the TV screen is just the physical part of what I do. It's a two-dimensional representation of a four-dimensional world.

People who don't understand the consequences of being possessed or having a demon follow you home think ghost hunting sounds like fun and therefore aren't afraid of it. Skeptics who don't believe that spirits exist are usually fearless of going on an investigation because they are convinced there's nothing out there (which makes a great litmus test. Take a skeptic on an investigation—if he's afraid, then he's really a believer).

The main hazard of this profession is encountering a spirit who does not want to let you go. As I've stated before, many spirits will stay with you once they know you can see or hear them. They become attracted to those who are in touch with the spiritual world, and even long after I've left the physical confines of an investigation, I will have a spirit following me around trying to make contact. That makes this a 24-7 job oftentimes, and it's usually not Caspar the Friendly Ghost hovering over my shoulder.

At home in Las Vegas, I've had four girlfriends attacked by spirits after paranormal investigations (especially after Bobby Mackey's Music World). Maybe they're jealous. Maybe they're protective. Maybe it's the succubus coming for me and pushing them aside. I don't know, but they always go after my girlfriends in a bad way. That makes having a relationship difficult, especially when combined with the violent nightmares I get, like the one in London. Nightmares frequently happen the night after a lockdown and though they usually fade with time, this isn't always the case.

Demon attacks are probably the worst danger. Not only is the physical attack painful and scary, but the blood transfer between the human and the demon can have permanent effects as well. I actually had to have a minor exorcism performed on me after my third investigation of Bobby Mackey's Music World. Thankfully this doesn't happen often or I'd have to get some kind of special demon protection insurance. No one offers that, so staying strong with the spirits is the only thing that protects me. I try very hard to not show fear in front of them because if they perceive me as being weak, then they'll try to push me around. Active taunting is a strategy I reserve for certain types of spirits, but no matter what, I never back down.

Beyond the mental hazards of paranormal investigation, there are the physical dangers of entering dilapidated buildings teeming with black mold, asbestos, and even homeless vagrants. I've had pneumonia and bronchitis several times, and it's not fun. I now take every possible protective measure I can to avoid situations like those, such as wearing protective masks and walking through a building in the daylight to identify hazards. Injuries are always possible in abandoned buildings. There's usually debris everywhere that can twist an ankle, fall on you in the dark, or jump out and surprise you. I've run into doors, support columns, and even a steel bar across a cell door at Eastern State Penitentiary.

Sometimes the worst hazard is getting what you asked for. Back at the Amargosa Hotel and Opera House in Death Valley, I was taunting the Boss Man when he answered my challenge with a strike of his own.

"If you're the nasty spirit that likes to push people, I hate bullies," I said. "Come and face me. Bring it!"

Suddenly a voice came from the Boss Man's room. "All the lights are off," I heard without the need for a digital recorder. Minutes later I was coughing uncontrollably, light headed, dizzy, and unable to get myself right. I strongly believe I was being channeled by the Boss Man. It went deep, making me feel physically sick like a dying patient in Amargosa's old mining hospital. But instead of trying to contact me, he was trying to hurt me.

In the movie *Powder*, the main character grabs a dying deer in one hand and grabs a man with his other, transferring the pain of the suffering animal to the human. Like that, I feel the Boss Man was grabbing me and making me feel the pain and suffering he or his victim experienced. Was I feeling black lung from a suffering miner? Was I feeling the last breaths of a suffocating patient?

"Something is really wrong with my body," I said to Aaron and Nick.

"No one cares," came a disembodied response. He was mocking me, but no matter how hard angry spirits like him push, I won't back down. If I did, the bullies would win.

That's not happening.

ADMINISTRATION

SECTION
V
Evil

Pennhurst.

Move to the sound of the guns." It's an old army saying that basically means "if you hear gunfire, march toward it instead of run away from it." Soldiers should always get into the fight, not go in the opposite direction. In paranormal investigation I move to the sound of the ghosts. At Pennhurst Hospital I heard a loud bang when the building was abandoned. It startled me, but while most people would run away from it, I ran toward it. It's the knowledge that a spirit just manifested and took action that makes me run to wherever it just happened and explore it. If I ran away, what kind of "investigator" would I be?

Sure there are spirits who intentionally try to harm the living and running headlong into them can sometimes be foolhardy, but those are also the ones that get me excited. I don't know why, but I live to fight the truly evil entities on their own grounds and always look for ways to defeat them. I get very angry when I think of the evil spirits and demons that want to harm the living, and instead of shying away from the challenge, I welcome it.

Mean Spirits

Why are there spirits who want to harm the living? Why do they want to cause us pain and suffering? Why are there spirits who seek to drive us crazy with malicious, taunting behavior? The answers to these questions have huge implications on the paranormal because proving that these evil entities exist shows that our identities cross over with us after death. If a person was a bully who took sick pleasure in hurting others in life and continues to do so in death, then that shows intelligence and personality exists in the afterlife. If an asshole in life is an asshole in death, then to me that's proof positive that our identities cross over with us. It also provides a glimpse into the plane they exist in, because it shows that emotion and intent are trapped with them between this world and the next. So in a way, evil spirits strengthen my belief in the existence of ghosts probably more than good spirits do.

I've run across many mean spirits (and yes, there is a difference between mean and evil that I'll get into soon). The first time I ran into one I was taken aback, because I really wasn't sure what I was getting into. I wanted to believe that all the spirits of the dead had found some sort of rapturous closure and felt some sort of peace after death. After all, we all want to believe that death brings peace and our souls become one with the universe. I found out the hard way that this is not the case.

There are, without a doubt, mean spirits who want your body to feel physical pain and your mind to be plagued by mental anguish. They're not satisfied with merely scratching you or throwing something at you. They want something more. They want to use your own fears against you and cause long-term psychological damage and grief counseling. Their lives are over and their afterlives are miserable, so they want to ruin ours as a final "screw you" to the world they've left behind. They're cowardly and get me riled up if you couldn't tell. What's important to remember when encountering spirits like this is that they do not have any special powers. They cannot lift an axe and chop you to pieces or shoot laser beams from their dead eyes. They're former human beings and are limited to only those actions that a normal spirit has. I say this because investigators like me have to keep it in mind or our fears will run wild and get in the way of conducting a proper investigation and finding answers.

The Goldfield Hotel in Goldfield, Nevada, was my baptism

by fire into the paranormal world. It's the place where I made my documentary film with Nick Groff and had the infamous encounter with a flying brick that to this day is one of *the best* pieces of paranormal evidence ever captured on film. It's where I grew from curious Zak to professional Zak in the blink of an eye and where I realized that this shit is real. The Goldfield Hotel taught me a lot about not walking into a haunted location unprepared. But most importantly, it's where I learned that evil walks the Earth and my destiny is to fight it.

Two years after the flying brick incident (and remember it wasn't just a brick—boards and other debris levitated in a whirlwind of poltergeist activity), some fellow paranormal friends joined Aaron, Nick, and me in a trip back to the Goldfield Hotel with 100 people to conduct a public investigation. We did this event partly because of the controversy that ensued after we publicized our shocking evidence. We were hoping for some kind of similar activity to occur and be witnessed by people we'd never met before to verify that this place was a hotbed of unexplained activity.

We split up, with me taking thirty people upstairs to the fourth floor to conduct EVP sessions and use provoking techniques to entice the spirits in the building to make their presence known. I lined my guests up down the main hallway, stood at one end and started provoking the spirits. "Show yourselves. Show these people that you're real," I demanded. "Show them what you did to us when we were here! Come out here and let us know you're real."

At the opposite end of the hall I heard a screech followed by another one. For a moment I feared I had gone too far and caused a malevolent spirit to harm a guest. An uneasy nausea came over me as I ran toward the commotion. Once there I was stunned by what was happening. Several small rocks on the ground were being levitated vertically and thrown horizontally at an older gentleman at the end of the hall, pelting him several times. At the same time all of his electronic equipment (a digital recorder and a video camera) went dead. This was the biggest reward; having all these people witness this. This is what we were waiting for!

At the same time that this happened the hotel's caretaker, Virginia Ridgeway (who also appeared in our documentary), had an experience that she would never forget and still blames me for. As I was asking the spirits to move something and my tone escalated, Virginia claims two dark shadow figures entered the room she was in and attacked her. She was (allegedly) lifted off the ground and thrown against a wall. She shrieked, so we immediately rushed her out of the building to recover. I remember she was extremely shaken up as if something had really traumatized her.

Did you know? Later we learned that this was not Virginia Ridgeway's first dark encounter in the hotel. Virginia had been physically lifted off the floor and slammed into a wall near room 109 while witnessing a cleansing ceremony (that included a pentagram drawn on the floor) long before I ever met her. I do not take responsibility for the encounter that happened during our event, since we all knew this building was occupied by some very dark entities and Virginia knew the risks of going into it better than anyone.

The flying pebbles were bizarre and frightening because we were still new to the paranormal world and I wasn't sure how to react to such aggressive activity. I wasn't sure if I should thank the spirits for responding to my challenge or chastise them for being mean. Things like this happen around me a lot nowadays, but back then I was still a babe in the woods and had yet to get comfortable with spirits throwing objects at my request and trying to hurt my guests. After all, these people were my responsibility. I was leading this party.

I remember the people who witnessed that remarkable event came up to Nick and me afterward and thanked us with tears in their eyes. "This is why I traveled twelve hours in my car," they said. "I didn't think this stuff was real, but you guys showed me the truth." That was very rewarding, but I had to disagree some. "We didn't show you," I said. "They showed you." I felt like Ray in the movie *Field of Dreams* when only he and his family could see the ghosts in his cornfield. Then finally that one moment came when everyone could see them. The smile on Kevin Costner's face was my smile, but it wasn't in a fictional movie.

After the flying pebble incident, we weren't allowed to investigate the Goldfield Hotel. The owner was unhappy with us and refused to return any calls. The only building in the town that we were allowed to investigate was the Nixon building across the street, which we were preparing for one day in 2010 when fate stepped in.

Goldfield is like that town in *The Hills Have Eyes*. It's quiet, small, and just plain strange. As we arrived in town for the Nixon building investigation we saw Red Roberts, the owner of the Goldfield Hotel, standing in the street with his truck parked in front of the hotel. This was a huge opportunity because for years he had avoided us and we had no clue why.

Seeing Red was too random for me to accept as coincidence. He very rarely travels to Goldfield, despite owning the largest structure in town. He lives in Carson City and was there working on a door in the hotel, so seeing him standing in the street just as we arrived for only the third time in six years was fate.

Nick and I immediately ran up to him. "Do you remember

us?" I asked before he could get away.

"Yeah I remember you guys," he responded in that, "oh crap" sort of way. It was clear he was not thrilled to see us.

Convincing him to allow us back into the hotel was like selling caffeine to a Mormon. He wasn't going for it, and I couldn't understand why. We eventually learned that our film had made the Goldfield too popular. Our documentary made the place a favorite for paranormal investigators everywhere, which unfortunately also brought with it vandalism and made Red reluctant to let anyone inside. Finally Red relented and told us to see Virginia Ridgeway, the caretaker who lived nearby and would let us inside, but she was another problem.

Unbeknown to me at the time, Virginia was mad at me for the attack by the two dark shadows during the pebble incident. While our attention was on the man who was the target of the pebble attack, two dark shadows pushed Virginia up against a wall and bruised her. In the years since that incident, she had been attacked by evil entities several more times inside the hotel and at her home, just a two-minute walk from the hotel. She was convinced our investigation made the spirits inside darker and more evil. She'd never needed an escort in the building or been afraid to go inside alone before, but after our pebble incident, she'd been hesitant to even enter it. I hate to think that my actions caused evil spirits to take revenge on an elderly woman, but it appears that's what they did. But as I said earlier, I can't ignore the fact that she was attacked by the spirits there before I even stepped foot in that building.

What's odd to me is that some people go into the hotel for one night and come out terrified, but Red Roberts goes in there by himself continuously and nothing happens to him. It's like he has a deal with them to back off and in return he keeps the hotel standing. He's like a clownfish living in a poisonous anemone that never gets stung. I think Red knows something about the darkness in there that he'll take to the grave with him, which sounds eerily familiar to another demon-infested building in Kentucky and an owner who refuses to believe in what's happening there.

But hold that thought.

We finally got our investigation and once again ran headlong into the mean and nasty souls hanging out in the Goldfield Hotel (just as a side note—if I were going to pick a place to hang out in the afterlife it sure as hell wouldn't be in Goldfield, Nevada). One of the most ironic and eerie paranormal events that I've ever had happen to me occurred during this investigation. I was talking about the flying pebble incident when a rock flew at us and hit Nick in the back. The rock's trajectory was parallel to the ground and came up the stairs from below, so we easily debunked it as not being anything natural (like debris falling from the ceiling).

Are you freaking kidding me? As I'm describing the flying rocks, a new rock gets thrown at us? Now if that does not show intelligent, malicious intent, then I don't know what does. I really think it was an attempt by the spirits there to hurt us and even if the rock was not thrown with a lot of force, it was (at the very least) an attempt to hurt us psychologically. What better way is there for a spirit to say, "fuck you" than to do the exact thing that you're talking about at the moment you say it? It's a way for them to make a statement like "this is our turf and we're in control here." Since I'm a bit of a control freak and like being in charge, I took this rock and their challenge a little personally.

Another nasty spirit whose behavior I took a little personally is called "Mister Boots" and he's got an attitude like his long lost brother, Mister Scrooge. Boots hangs out in the seedy section of one of the most oddly attractive places I've ever been: Edinburgh, Scotland. The Edinburgh Vaults are a maze of catacombs beneath the city that has experienced a torrent of death and turmoil over its 223-year history. I really like Wikipedia's description of the place:

The Edinburgh Vaults or South Bridge Vaults are a series of chambers formed in the nineteen arches of the South Bridge in Edinburgh, Scotland, which was completed in 1788. For around 30 years, the vaults were used to house taverns, cobblers and other tradesmen, and as storage space for illicit material, reportedly including the bodies of people killed by serial killers Burke and Hare for medical experiments.

As the conditions in the vaults deteriorated, mainly because of damp and poor air quality, the businesses left and the very poorest of Edinburgh's citizens moved in, though by around 1820, even they are believed to have left too. That people had lived there was only discovered in 1985 during an excavation, when middens were found containing toys, medicine bottles, plates, and other signs of human habitation.

Nice!

One room of the vaults was designated as the former dwelling place of Mister Boots, the spirit of a particularly nasty soul who supposedly wears thigh-high boots. I hear those were fashionable in his day, but it's hard not to think of them as groovy and somewhat unmanly. When his room was discovered, the skeleton of a woman, believed to be a prostitute whom Boots killed and kept for himself, was also found, so it's very possible that Mister Boots was a murdering, philandering piece of filth.

We heard Mister Boots didn't like people in his room, and our guide told us to keep our lights off so as not to anger him, so turning my light on was the first thing I did. Like I said, I don't like bullies. I also felt like the guides were hamming it up, so I decided to call their bluff. After all, I get my best evidence when I'm provoking spirits.

After dark, I went into Mister Boots's room and did everything the guide told us not to do. I provoked and prodded and said things that probably weren't nice, but that's the best way to get a reaction out of spirits like this one—by challenging them. In life Mister Boots was most likely an alpha male, the dominant person in his little circle with no real rivals. He was probably not challenged much, so he doesn't take kindly to someone like me walking into his home and spewing unsavory comments at him. That's the theory when it comes to spirits like him, and in this case, it was right.

Within a few minutes I felt a presence and heard disembodied voices around me. You have to remember—while you're at home chilling comfortably on your couch watching this stuff on your flat-screen TV, eating a Lunchable and stacking the cheese on your cracker sandwich, you can't *feel* what it's like to actually be in the company of one of these nasty spirits. It is the unnerving feeling that you've momentarily lost control of the situation. It's not just hearing a scratch on the wall. It's like taking your *Avatar* umbilical cord and attaching it to a serial killer who is serving five life sentences in the solitary unit at San Quentin Prison. You *feel* their energy, and you don't have a choice but to accept it. It's like being held underwater by an invisible force and panicking because you don't know what the fuck is going on.

Seconds later, the loudest scratching noise I'd ever heard raked across the walls, like Freddy Kruger's claws on corrugated tin. Now, this place was dark. Most times I'll have a little ambient light to work with on an investigation, but the Edinburgh Vaults were darker than the bottom of the ocean, so the scratch and the energy that penetrated me at the same time really startled me. I jumped and instantly regretted it, but like I've said before, fear is hard to control in these situations.

I'm sure the noises I heard were the reactions of Mister Boots. I was an intruder in his world, so he lashed out every way he knew how. It was the reaction I wanted, and though it startled me, I can't complain. I was asking for it.

For the skeptics who ask why I don't do more debunking I have this to say—what do you want me to do? In the Edinburgh Vaults I heard a clear scratching sound on the walls, but there was no one in the room with me. I can pick up an object and scrape it against the wall to replicate the sound, but that doesn't debunk the incident. I can do a lot of things to make a similar sound, but that does not disprove the evidence as being caused by something natural. It only proves that I could grab a metal object and scrape it down a wall.

Nasty spirits like Mister Boots intrigue me a lot and are one of the main reasons I do this job. I love the feeling of throwing nastiness back at the mean spirit who thinks the living cannot do anything to him. Many times these spirits are like bullies who just want to push someone around and think they cannot be pushed back. So when I show up and surprise them with provocation and challenging, it can change their demeanor and even change their behavior so they leave the living alone—for a while at least. That's rewarding.

The dungeon located in the secret, hidden room under my house.

Hanging Out with Vampires

While in Edinburgh we investigated Greyfriars Cemetery and just before going there we interviewed Kryss, a man who looked like the dude from *The Crow*, all dressed up in black leather and piercings. He told us a story of how he was a vampire, which we didn't think much of, but it ended up being one of the weirdest encounters I've ever had. Everywhere we went Kryss would be there, walking by himself in the distance and staring at us. It was stalkerish, or something out of *The Hitcher*, where the weird guy in the trench coat is always over your shoulder.

One night after the investigation he invited Aaron and I out to an underground bar that was actually set inside one of the Edinburgh Vaults. It was a dark, gothic place that you would think I would feel right at home in, but instead it had the opposite effect—it creeped me out, which is saying a lot, since I have my own dungeon in my house. We met Kryss and his four friends who were also dressed very dark, like the people in *Thirty Days to Night*. All of them worked at an armory or a sword shop. They were not normal.

Well, in this group of four they had one overweight kid whom they beat up like it was a recreational activity. We were sitting in the bar and they would just start hitting him in the body and even in the face. It was a very awkward, and just to make things weirder these people told Aaron and me they were vampires, but instead of feeding on blood, they fed on sex.

Officially freaked out.

There are situations where good friends don't need to speak to understand each other. I looked at Aaron and he looked at me and we both knew it was time to get away. We walked to the bar and looked back at our booth. There they were, sitting in their black leather clothes, under the misty green light like the bar in *Blade*, beating up their fat mascot. We didn't want to be rude and leave, but we were definitely not comfortable in the situation, so we decided to make a run for it. We walked out into the street and I swear they were out there waiting for us.

"Where are you going?" one asked.

What. The. Hell?

I muttered something lame like, "I was just checking my watch." They didn't buy it. We thought we were getting turned into vampires or stunned, weaved into a web, and made into giant tarantula food. We accompanied them to another bar just because we were scared not to. There was no choice.

Could things get any stranger? Yep.

At the next bar, they told us about the island they lived on and how they were embroiled in a bitter vampire war with a rival vampire gang from Italy. They asked us to go to their island so they could turn us into vampires too. It's ironic that a guy like me, who's always been enamored with vampires and the supernatural, was uncomfortable around people who claimed to be just what I was.

I once saw a documentary on Weird Al Yankovic and was convinced he had the strangest fans in the world. Not anymore.

Territorial Spirits

This is mine and that's yours. It's a basic rule of society. We have fences, property lines, borders, and even firewalls on our computers to keep the unwanted out and protect the things we have. When it comes to our loved ones the protection gets even more rabid and emotional. Ever hear the phrase "don't mess with a momma bear's cubs?" It's true. A parent can be downright violent and deadly when it comes to the protection of their offspring. Lovers can be hyperprotective, especially when jealousy or the thought of losing control over a mate is involved. How many times have you heard those stories about a man who keeps his girl too close because he's terrified of losing her?

That willingness to protect a loved one can carry over into the spirit world. I've seen it several times. At Bobby Mackey's Music Hall in Wilder, Kentucky, we caught an EVP of a spirit saying, "Precious . . . no." I'm convinced it was a male spirit holding back a female spirit and possibly the disembodied voice of Scott Jackson trying to keep his former lover Pearl Bryan from contacting us. Scott Jackson (a known devil worshipper) was convicted and executed for the murder of Bryan, who was pregnant at the time. On the gallows swore he would haunt Mackey's.

If this was Jackson talking to Bryan, what was he trying to stop her from doing? Was he afraid of her contacting me? Was he afraid of losing her? There are so many possible scenarios when an EVP like this is captured that I have to stop myself from obsessing over it. Who is Precious? Who is the man trying to stop her and why? This is my conflict, my drama, and my gossip. The paranormal is my *Desperate Housewives, Survivor,* and *Ultimate Fighter* rolled into one.

The worst case of good and evil locking horns that I've experienced was at the Villisca Axe Murder House in Villisca, Iowa. Built in 1868, this quaint southern Iowa home is nothing extraordinary. If you didn't know a hideous crime had been committed there, it would be an ideal prairie home in a tight knit community where everyone knows everyone. It was bought by Joe Moore and his family in 1903, and became infamous in 1912 when Joe, his wife, their four children, and two visiting children were all found hacked to death in their beds one morning. It was a grisly crime that caught the attention of the country and, of course, fueled ghost stories for almost a century.

Though there were several suspects, the killer was never caught, and all suspects are now long dead themselves. William Mansfield, an ex-con, seems to be the most likely killer. His own wife, his infant daughter, and his in-laws were murdered by an axe in Blue Island, Illinois, two years later using the same techniques as the Villisca murders. Similar axe murders had occurred in Kansas and Colorado, to which Mansfield could be connected too, but he was never convicted of any of them. Another suspect was a drifter and possible schizophrenic named Andy Sawyer, who was arrested and questioned for the murders, but released.

I'd like to think that what the justice system could not discover, we did. In the middle of the night, when there's nothing left but you, the spirits, and the darkness, the truth can be found if you know where to look.

"Who killed you?" I asked, waiting in the silence. Moments later when I reviewed the digital recording of the Spirit Box, I got a response that I did not expect.

"Andy."

I think one of the spirits, probably Joe Moore, knew Andy Sawyer and knows he was responsible for killing his family. I also think he does not want his deceased family to know they are dead and is keeping that information from them because during the night we also got another revealing EVP.

"We're gonna keep them in the dark," a voice said, "'Cause they don't step in heaven yet."

This was certainly an intelligent spirit who was responding to our questions on the upper floor. It was one of the best full-sentence EVPs I ever caught, and it fit perfectly with the lore of the house.

So is it possible that a spirit can still reside in a building and hold back other spirits that also reside there? Can one spirit keep information from the others that are also trapped in the building? Can one spirit prevent others from crossing over to the other side? Can he prevent them from getting closure? Eight people were killed in the Villisca Axe Murder House. Six of them were children and two were adults. Is it possible that those adults are still looking after the kids, keeping them away from intruders like me? The big question is why would they do this. Could they be unwilling to let go of their family and this is their last attempt to keep them together in death?

Maybe there's another layer to this mystery. Maybe the spirit of the killer has returned and that's really who Joe Moore is protecting his family from. We've seen in the past that spirits can return to a place of extreme emotional attachment, even if it's a long way from where they died. Another EVP we caught seems to suggest this might be the case.

"Do you know who killed you?" Aaron asked in the basement.

"They're upstairs," a voice responded. Whoever was upstairs, the spirit that contacted Aaron seemed afraid of it. Maybe it was the spirit of the man who had committed this heinous deed, who had returned to the scene of the crime and was now terrorizing the family again.

Good and evil spirits are definitely at odds in Villisca, and the energy there is very strong. Paranormal energy has been recorded by so many groups that it's impossible to discount that the spirits of the dead still reside there. But why do we capture both good and evil EVPs and poltergeist activity in the same building? Why is there a fight going on inside the house on a plane that we cannot see? Is it possible that these killings were not the product of a psychopath, but were triggered by an evil that sprang up to possess William Mansfield, Andy Sawyer, or whoever the killer was? Is it possible that the killer was possessed by an evil entity that left its host once the crimes were done? These are the questions that keep me up at night.

You can read about a place like Villisca all you like, but it's not until you walk through the door, talk to the people who lived there, and feel the torment inside that you realize how heavy a place like this is. A family that once lived in this house as kids couldn't even return to it, and when we interviewed them, they shook with fear and had to step outside. Up until that investigation I'd never experienced a possession personally, and I have to admit, I was hoping to at Villisca. It didn't happen, but I wouldn't have to wait long.

Weird coincidence—One day after writing this passage I received a message from a friend that the owner of the Villisca Axe Murder House and huge GAC supporter, Darwin, passed away. You will be missed, my friend. Rest in Peace.

The Island of Rage

Poveglia. The name still haunts me. Looking at it from the nearby island of Venice, where millions of people lounge away their European vacations cruising a gondola through the Grand Canal, you would not think of it as being so hideous. But this quiet island in Northern Italy is as sinister a place as has ever existed on Earth and has seen hundreds of thousands of death in its long and tortured history. Naturally it's considered one of the ultimate places of paranormal energy and calls out to investigators like me with an unavoidable power. But this black hole of evil, which could have been a pleasant little brother to the legendary Venice, is not for the weak or casual traveler. Here are the highlights of its dark history:

During the days of the Roman Empire it was allegedly used to isolate victims of the black plague. That set a bad precedent that would be repeated many times over. In 1379 Venice was one of the most powerful societies in the world. It was a light at the end of the tunnel known as the dark ages and had everything going for it. Suddenly it was under attack (again) from the neighboring city of Genoa and its powerful navy, so the people living on Poveglia (there were a lot by then) were moved to Giudecca to protect them. In their place the Venetian government built a permanent fortification called "the Octagon" on the island to help keep the Genoese navy away. The Octagon is still visible today.

The island was reportedly uninhabited during the fifteenth century, though I cannot find a reason why. In the sixteenth century, a plague outbreak ravaged Italy, and with an empty island sitting just a few miles away, it was an easy decision to transform Poveglia into a quarantine facility (also called a *lazaretto*).

After all, no one wanted the place, so why not keep the unwanted there, especially since most of Venice's economy depended on trade and people from all over the world traveled through it? This move probably helped save Venice from experiencing a lot of death, but it also made Poveglia an island of hell.

For a long time Poveglia was empty, so in 1527 the Venetians offered the island to a group of monks, who refused to take it. Bad omen. In 1661 the Venetians offered to reconstruct a village for the descendants of the original inhabitants of Poveglia, but they also refused the offer. You would think a free island with a rebuilt village is an offer you can't refuse, but they did. Another good call. The Venetian government was getting the hint that no one wanted to live there.

By 1805 most of Italy was under the iron fist of Napoleon, and under his rule Poveglia (the island that no one wanted) became a *lazaretto* again during a new outbreak of plague. This lasted until 1814. During these Napoleonic wars, it is said that the English occupied the island, ambushed French ships, and burned the crews alive on Poveglia. The last time anyone made an attempt to use the island was in 1922. Its buildings were converted into a hospital that housed both the insane and the homeless, but by 1969 it was completely abandoned.

So Poveglia was a magnet for suffering and death. Hundreds of thousands of people (that's right, hundreds of thousands) died on its soil from plague, war, tsunami, mental illness, suicides, and executions. It's the perfect storm for darkness, death, dread, and murder. Locals say half the island is made from the ashes of the dead who were burned and buried there, which I can somewhat verify. As I stabbed my machete into the soil, it penetrated it like a hot knife in butter. It wasn't sand. It wasn't soil. And it wasn't dirt. It was ash.

Where does the raw energy from all these tormented souls

Poveglia . . . The plague . . . The doctor.

go? I mentioned before that people abruptly killed while caught in a whirlwind of emotion (anger, rage, excitement, agony) are unable to cross over to their final plane. Their energy is still in chaos, and they have to wander the Earth until that energy is put at rest. We all generally believe spirits of the departed need to be put at rest. It makes us uncomfortable to think there is no peace after death, so RIP (Rest In Peace) has become a common wish in English for the departed. I experienced that wandering energy pass through in the middle of the night. It was exhilarating, terrifying, and overwhelming.

I personally think Poveglia is infested by an evil that manipulates the living. I don't think the English would have killed so many French sailors if they had been on any other island. I believe an evil calls Poveglia home and causes the spirits there to know nothing but negative emotions. They can do a few things: they can manipulate the human spirits on the island, they can manipulate the humans who visit it, or they can take it to a new level and try to possess humans like me who visit. I think this is what happened. I was being influenced by the angry and evil spirits of Poveglia like the devil's marionette. Once you set foot on this island you have fallen into a whirlpool to hell. You either swim your way out or get sucked deeper and deeper into the control of the only current it has—evil.

I don't call what happened to me in that place a possession, at least not in the literal sense of the term. We're a society that's been affected heavily by pop culture and the media. People think a possession means your head spins around, you puke green bile, and you suddenly have the ability to walk on the ceiling. I can tell you that I don't know anyone that this has happened to.

Possession by a spiritual being, either human or animal, is something almost every religion has accepted for centuries. Roman Catholic doctrine states that angels are non-corporeal beings, purely spiritual creatures that have intelligence and will. Fallen angels, or demons, are able to "demonically possess" individuals without the victim's knowledge or consent, so they are not responsible for their actions while being possessed. Possession can last for as little as a few minutes or as long as several months.

Funny fact—all Catholic churches are required to have a demonologist on their staff. That indicates an acceptance that they exist.

More on possession in a minute. First let's finish the story of Poveglia. I don't remember everything that happened to me that night. I know we were in the main hospital of Poveglia trying to lure the spirits out. Nick was chanting over and over, *Risotta lo mia energia*, which means "Use my energy" in Italian.

Next thing I know, I felt different. And not just a little different. I felt like someone else was looking through my eyes. Nothing looked familiar to me. I froze. My body wouldn't move. I looked at Aaron and suddenly felt a rage build up in me to do him harm. I saw myself tearing him apart. I wanted to peel his skin off and gouge out his eyes.

"Get out of here!" I yelled, lashing out for no apparent reason. I squeezed the camera in my hands until it snapped. For a second I thought I might be having a stroke or some sort of super-bad reaction to shellfish, but there was no way this was anything like that. An anger took me over and the fight was on. I fought to get whatever it was in me out. It was a struggle between good and evil that I eventually won, but not before going through a traumatic battle. I had to keep reminding myself who I was, and that I wasn't weak enough to be taken over or evil enough to hurt my friends. I had to concentrate on all the good things in my life until the darkness left me.

After I shouted at Aaron, he wisely left me alone. Nick also moved away from me and went behind a wall until it was over. What was really dangerous was that I had a machete on my hip at the time. We had been using it to get through some of the thick over grown weeds on the island. Luckily the evil trying to take me over didn't realize it. If it had . . .

I had a hard time watching the footage when we got home. Afterward I didn't want the entire episode to air because I didn't want my niece and nephew to see me like that. It was scary. It just wasn't me. I grabbed at Aaron and yelled at him more than what was shown on the episode. I didn't speak in audible words, but garbled and mumbly tones instead. It lasted a lot longer than you would think too. It was about an hour between the time I first felt strange until I got back to my senses. All I really remember is doing a cleansing afterward with a sacred chrism on my forehead and feeling like it was hot grease burning the evil energy away.

What I learned from that incident was to pay attention to the warning signs. Several things happened before I was taken over. There were footsteps echoing down the hallways. Aaron got a sudden and massive headache. We'd had an unusually high EMF reading, and I just wasn't feeling like myself. Looking back on it, it all added up, but I still didn't expect anything like that to happen. I've never experienced anything like it before or since. In my right mind I would never treat Aaron that way. He's one of my best friends, and I apologized to him later—a few times.

In a sick way I can't say that I didn't enjoy it. My mission in life is to make contact with the souls of the deceased, whether they're the nice, innocent kind or the smelly, evil ones. It's my job to understand these spirits, find out what makes them tick, and come up with ways to communicate with them. So I have to accept it as a hazard of the job when I come across a bad apple, even if he wants to harm me. I have to get into their world and come up with answers, no matter what their intentions are.

It wasn't my first profound experience with a demon, but it was a significant one that left me wanting to know more. When our time in Poveglia was done, I went down to another room and avoided leaving. But today the encounter still haunts me a little. Someday I'll go back there. Someday.

Hell's Gate

Only one other place infiltrates me like Poveglia Island, and for good reason. If there's a portal to another dimension of dark, malevolent energy in this world, it is undoubtedly the former abandoned slaughterhouse on the banks of the Licking River in Wilder, Kentucky, called Bobby Mackey's Music World. I've investigated it three times and each time I discover a new layer of hell. I first went there in 2008 and was shocked by the ominous warning over the front door that cannot be avoided.

"This place is reportedly haunted. Enter at your own risk. Not responsible for demon attacks."

Oh mama. The bar was ordered to display this sign by the local courts after Bobby Mackey's was sued for an attack by an evil spirit on a patron. Yes, this really happened. This place is no bullshit.

Paranormal activity didn't start the minute I walked through the door of Mackey's, but it didn't take long for the ghouls to get stirred up. It seemed that everywhere we went voices whispered

Mackey's . . .
Standing on the well from hell.

and the sounds of movement echoed throughout the establishment—behind the stage, around the corner from the bar, under the tables. It was like elves were scurrying about in the shadows watching us and laughing at us for wanting to be there alone and at night. This was their world, and we were the guests. We were minnows in a shark tank, but that's also the way we like it, because this is where the fight-or-flight instinct kicks in. I was threatened on all sides, and like any human who believes in self-preservation, I was on edge. These are the moments where people have to make the tough decision between standing and running. There was no way I was going to run.

When you hear the history of Mackey's it's easy to see why people pray to an almighty God before stepping across its threshold. I love what I do and I voluntarily go into the places most won't, but Mackey's is different. Since its opening as a country music bar, twenty-nine affidavits of demonic events have been filed against the establishment and hundreds more undocumented incidents have occurred to those too scared to talk about it. Bobby Mackey's own wife hated the place and refused to set foot in it after having her head mysteriously shoved into a sink as she washed dishes and then being thrown down a set of stairs. When Mackey's wife reached the bottom of the stairs and looked up, she saw the face of her assailant and later matched it to an old drawing of Alonzo Walling.

Walling and his cohort, Scott Jackson, were convicted of the murder of Jackson's girlfriend, Pearl Bryan in 1896. After killing Pearl they decapitated her, performed a satanic ritual in the bowels of the building (which was then a slaughterhouse), and discarded Pearl's head in the well that carried animal blood to the Licking River. On the gallows, Alonzo Walling and Scott Jackson swore they'd haunt the building forever. It seems they kept that promise.

But that's just the beginning of the establishment's dark history. Before Mackey converted it to a country and western nightclub, it was a speakeasy during the time of prohibition, a roadhouse for the transients and travelers of Kentucky's by-ways, a casino run by organized crime, and a nightclub that was shut down because of several fatal shootings. During its days as a casino, one of the establishment's singers, Robert Randall, got his girlfriend, Johanna, pregnant. When her mobster father found out, he killed Randall and in a fit of emotional retribution, Johanna poisoned her father before taking her own life.

There are many more stories that would take up a lot more pages, but I think you get the point. The building has a long and comfortable relationship with violence, death, and darkness, and it even got bad enough that an exorcism was performed on the entire place in 1994. Three years prior to that a personal exorcism was performed on the one man who was nearly killed by the evil inside Bobby Mackey's, Carl Lawson.

Carl never intended to be possessed (and who does really?). He was the caretaker of Bobby Mackey's who lived in an apartment above the bar and was charged with managing the building and repairing anything that needed fixing. Even a short stay in Bobby Mackey's is enough to drive good men bad, so living in the place full time is enough to get you a custom-fitted straightjacket.

Carl had heard all the tales. He knew the well had once been used for satanic rituals. Some of the local folks referred to it as "Hell's Gate." Although he wasn't very religious, Carl decided to sprinkle some holy water on the old well one night, thinking that it might bring some relief from the spirits. Bad idea. Instead, it seemed to awaken them and the paranormal activity in the building suddenly went off the charts. It's like a page right out of the movie *The Ring*.

After living in the building for several months, Carl Lawson was fully possessed by demonic forces in 1991. There are entire books written about Carl's possession that are truly terrifying. I'm not sure how long the possession lasted but Carl was only released after a six-hour exorcism by Reverend Glen Cole in 1991. If you've ever seen the video of the exorcism, it's disturbing. To this day Carl has the thousand-yard stare of someone who has stood on the edge of the abyss and somehow lived to tell about it.

That night we entered the Gates of Hell.

During the first investigation, I went upstairs to spend time in Johanna's former room. I was attempting to connect with the dancer's spirit when I heard a very loud thud downstairs. Aaron, who was on the main level at the time, and I rushed to the sound to find Nick out of breath and scared. It turned out that while Nick was in the men's room something slammed against the wall, sending him running out of the room. Whether the spirit threw an object against the wall or just used his energy to cause the sound, we were unsure, so we did what all good investigators do—we went to the site of the incident and challenged the spirit to do it again. This was also the site where a man was violently attacked by an evil spirit and later sued the establishment, causing the famous liability sign as you enter the building to be put up.

We did not get another thud, but we got a growl so demonic Nick instantly bolted for the door, which I was standing in at the time. Now, I was just as spooked as the guys were, but one thing I can't do is run. It's just not me. "Stop running!" I yelled at Nick as he tried to get past me. I wasn't trying to exert my control over Nick, but I think this kind of behavior is not what paranormal investigators should ever exhibit. It not only discredits us in front of the world, but also in front of the spirits

Bob Mackey's

we're trying to contact. If they see us running away, then why would they want to talk to us? Why would they respect us? We ran from something once before and I will never run again.

One of the hardest things to do as a paranormal investigator is keep your fear in check. It's always there. If it's not, then you're a nonbeliever because only those who believe in the paranormal and know the harm that it can cause are scared. Skeptics aren't scared because they don't believe there's anything out there that can harm them.

There has to be order and discipline during an investigation. I've been criticized in the past for being bossy with Aaron and Nick, but the truth is, I run a tight ship and feel that one person has to be the clear leader in these dark, eerie places or things go awry quickly. If that happens, then we don't accomplish all of our objectives and the investigation is a waste of time. I believe in efficiency and a clear chain of command . . . with me at the top of course.

At the same time that the thud hit the wall, we also heard something very eerie. A song very similar to "Three Blind Mice" was being hummed by an unseen voice. We were so preoccupied with the thud and trying to control ourselves that we didn't pay much attention to it at the time, but later we all recalled it and heard it when we played back our recorders. "Three Blind Mice." How weird is that? Who or what would find it entertaining to hum "Three Blind Mice" when we were in a state of mild panic? Could it be that demons have a sense of humor?

But the evil in Mackey's wasn't done with us yet. It's somewhat ironic that the worst physical attack by a spirit I've ever encountered was during one of my first investigations, but looking back on it now, it may also be the cause of some of the strange things that happen to me now. I was by the well in the basement doing my thing—pissing off evil ghosts (or so I thought)—when I felt a burning sensation on my back. This was no sunburn or mere poke, it was a stinging pain that ran from my neck to the small of my back. At first I didn't say anything, but moment by moment it got worse and eventually became very painful. Finally I asked the guys to look at it. I turned and Aaron lifted my shirt. When I heard him gasp, I knew something was wrong.

Three scratches, each one about ten to twelve inches long, streaked down my back. At one point they were deep enough to draw blood. We were still fairly new at PI, so I wasn't sure how to deal with this. All I knew is that it hurt and I was pissed, so I lashed out at the spirits, first with anger and then with taunting. Call me crazy, but I wanted more. I was already injured, so what more could they do? That's just me. When pushed, I push back.

Instead of leaving the building or retreating to a safe area, I took the fight to them and challenged them, though to be honest, I really didn't care to be scratched again. I was more interested in capturing something on tape or film, and the thought of engaging in some sort of blood exchange with a demon wasn't thrilling. Unfortunately, that was the culmination of paranormal activity in Bobby Mackey's that night. Everything went quiet, as if the demons there were satisfied with marking me and decided it was time to take a nap.

They may have been done for the night, but for me things were just starting. The mysterious marking I got that fateful evening was the moment everything changed, including me.

I returned to Bobby Mackey's with a group of friends in 2010 to conduct another investigation on our own without the support of the Travel Channel. For some reason I considered myself experienced enough that I believed nothing was going to happen to me. Turns out I was fooling myself because in the middle of the night, they found me again.

By this point I'd been on a lot of investigations where I'd been pushed and prodded by angry spirits, heard voices of disembodied souls, seen shadow apparitions, witnessed a full possession, and been attacked in some of the darkest places on Earth. Just like the first time I went to Mackey's, something happened the second time that I still can't explain.

The lower level of Mackey's is a catacomb for the decaying detritus of the former roadhouse/nightclub. It's lined with broken refrigerators, guitar cases, mattresses, discarded wood, and even an old weathervane. I was leading a small group of people through this downstairs area when Nick Groff interrupted us.

"Dude. You have to hear this," he said with an urgency in his voice as he held up his digital recorder. I've known Nick a long time and have been in many strange situations with him, so the raised eyebrows and perplexed look on his face told me he had something solid.

He played what he'd captured on his digital recorder, sending shivers down my spine. "Play that again," I said. When he did, we all distinctly heard "Hey guys. Be careful!" plain as any disembodied voice I'd ever captured—only this one was mine! It was my voice coming through the speaker. There was no doubting it.

"I've known you a long time, dude," Nick said, "and that is *your* voice."

He was right. It was my voice and I couldn't explain where it came from. I was saying words that I had not uttered that day, nor could I remember saying during the previous investigations of that building in the past. On top of that, we captured something else just as shocking.

One of our longtime fellow paranormal friends, Tara Bohren, was with us that evening. Just after my voice came through, her daughter's voice also crackled through the digital recorder, saying, "Mommy. Help." Understandably, Tara was upset and immediately moved away from the group to call home to ensure that her daughter was at home and in bed in Oregon. Another message that came through the shack hack that evening told Mark and Debby Constantino that their children were in a fire. They too immediately called home to make sure everyone was safe. I was befuddled, and as with any piece of evidence we capture, I was looking for an answer.

My initial attempt to explain this is to go to the source. I'm convinced demonic forces live in Bobby Mackey's Music Hall, and being evil, they enjoy toying with your emotions and causing you pain or confusion. I believe they achieve this by mimicking your voice, like they did with me. That definitely made me angry. And manipulating Tara by mimicking her daughter caused her emotional stress and set all of us off a little.

The taunting didn't stop there. Later that night we captured an eerie EVP that referred to me as "Z Man." That's what my father used to call me when I was a kid, and I hadn't heard it for many years. We heard it a few times on the ghost box and it certainly got my attention.

After that, the demons there shifted their focus and targeted Aaron. Disembodied voices picked at his failed marriage, and he changed in front of us. The always happy-go-lucky Aaron looked more like he was witnessing a family member being beaten. Something was wrong. He started to weep and then ran out of the room. I kept him separated from the group and together with a special guest we had with us, consoled him.

Bishop James Long is the Archbishop of the U.S. Old Catholic Church and is an expert in the field of demonology and exorcism. With all the crap that happened to us the first time around, I figured we could use an ace in the hole, especially since we were taking a large number of civilians into a profoundly evil place with us.

The bishop and I tried very hard to get Aaron under control and told him not to show fear. "Don't show weakness," we said repeatedly. "This is what they want. Stop crying." Things had, well, gone to hell—so fast that this was no longer a paranormal event. It was far more serious. It was a party with the devil. Aaron regained his senses, but after that one of my best friends started slipping away and changed dramatically. I think the evil there still has some strange control over him.

One more thing happened that night that was very profound and worth mentioning. In the basement we were doing an EVP when Bishop Long's recorder flew across the room and smashed. At the same time he felt a sharp fiery pain on his hand and when we looked at it, he was scratched across the back of his palm by three clear marks that were bleeding—just like the marks that were on my back a year before.

This is something that fascinates (and horrifies) me. Nearly every case of a physical demonic attack leaves the victim with three marks, as if the demon has a three-toed claw. Theologians believe this is the marking of the trinity—the Father, Son, and Holy Spirit. I think it's a sign that we're dealing with nonhuman forms. The three-toed mark also makes it easy to differentiate between a demonic attack and a self-inflicted wound. During our first investigation of Bobby Mackey's, I was attacked in the basement and had three long, painful scratches down my back.

This is how demons hurt us. They manipulate our skin and muscle to cause pain. Women feel penetration when an incubus enters the body. Men feel burning and usually end up with three scratch marks like I did the first time I was in Bobby Mackey's. The attack on the bishop was the same. It was the demon's attempt to hurt him by manipulation of his body. This attack confirmed that there was a demonic entity with us that evening, and whatever attacked the bishop was the same thing that had attacked me a year before.

All these incidents seemed to me like an attempt by the demons there to make us angry and cause us emotional pain. They enjoy watching us panic at the thought that our loved ones are being harmed. They're like bullies who get off on other people's misery and love to mimic your voice and mess with your mind. That's what makes a demon a demon instead of just a nasty or mean spirit and it's one of the reasons Bobby Mackey's is one of the darkest places on Earth.

A year later we returned to Bobby Mackey's for a third investigation (that's right—a third trip) and got even more than we bargained for. Bishop Long was with us again and almost immediately after entering the building he froze in his tracks. "An exorcism was performed here," he said to me near the kitchen. I stopped, unsure of what to say and looked at him. Just like my body tells me when ghosts are present, he could tell where an exorcism had taken place—and he was right. He did not catch it during the second investigation, but this time it was a powerful feeling that he couldn't miss.

A solemn rite of exorcism had been performed in that very spot years before. The solemn rite is serious business, and like ghosts, it leaves behind some sort of energy signature for guys like Bishop Long to pick up on.

He stood there for a long, awkward moment feeling the air and getting a sense of what he was up against. As he did so, I saw myself in him. I got a glimpse of what I must look like when I can feel a presence and I freeze to try to dial it in. His arms were outstretched and his senses were all on overdrive. Finally he moved away, but not before making a mental note of the location.

The solemn rite of exorcism that he sensed is no joke. It's the highest level of antidemonic incantation in the Catholic Church and is reserved for only the worst of the worst demonic entities. It's used only when a full possession has occurred and a place needs to be completely cleansed. What most people don't realize is that there are three levels of possession, all of which have their own "cures."

- The first level is an infestation. It's the lowest level and occurs when a demonic entity has made a nest in a building, but has not yet chosen a human body to reside in. Sometimes the demon intends to reside there without disturbing the humans it comes across and sometimes its intent is much more dastardly.
- The middle level is oppression. This is when a demon has chosen a human host and is trying to destroy its intellect and will. This is sometimes referred to as a transient stage when the demon is not fully in control of the human, but is trying to achieve it. To banish this level of demon, a priest like Bishop Long can perform a minor rite of exorcism.
- The highest level is full possession. At this point the demonic entity has full control of the human host and requires a solemn rite of exorcism to banish it. A demon can and will bring about death to its human host if it is not banished.

Knowing these levels of possession, I should have seen the signs of what was coming, but that's the difficulty of dealing with these beings—they can blind you and make it impossible to see what's happening around you.

More strange things happened during the night, so Bishop

Long decided the basement, where all the evil is centered, needed a full cleansing. The standard procedure in this situation is to go room to room and cleanse them (similar to what our military does when they clear a building). This corners the entity in the last room you go into and forces him to manifest. Once he exposes himself, the Bishop can banish him back to wherever he came from.

Suddenly we heard a loud and definite growl and knew that a clash was coming. It wasn't necessarily an animal, but an evil. It's important to note here that demons are not human sprits with bad intentions. According to the Catholic Church, an entity is either a demon *or* a human spirit, but not both. A human spirit cannot possess a living human. Demons are actually fallen angels with intelligence. At one time they were good, but for some reason they were sent back to Earth and turned dark. Demonic entities are not limited in their intensity, either. They don't have special powers, but do not have to rest like we do either.

Getting back to the exorcism, we were making progress through the basement when the demon tried to split the group up. We were clearing the rooms when I went into another room by myself and something happened that I still cannot explain. At this point I have to let Bishop Long tell the story since a lot of the details are still foggy to me (you'll hear why in a minute). All I really remember is that I was not myself. I remember someone took me by the hand and led me out to the well (I still don't recall who it was). They tell me I was talking in gibberish the whole way, but I don't remember it.

Bishop Long: "Zak's demeanor changed completely and I knew what was happening. I did some things to him to see if he was possessed or oppressed and determined he was not in a state of full possession. He was in a state of oppression, but

I had to act fast. The concern was no longer clearing the basement, but the health and welfare of Zak. It was time to leave the building, because remaining would have meant possession. The solemn rite is necessary for full possession, but this demon was still transient. He was still trying to gain control of Zak and use him as a human host. I performed an immediate blessing on Zak and a minor rite of exorcism to rid him of the evil. At this point the evening was no longer a paranormal investigation. I was worried about the people present. Any of them could go into a state of possession like what was happening to Zak, so we got everyone moved out of there."

Looking back on it, I can identify some mistakes we made. All of us were struggling on the inside with what was going on and not being vocal about it. We all had emotional issues, but held them in and tried to deal with them alone, which is always a bad idea. For Aaron, the spirit box kept saying personal things that affected him, but he kept quiet about it. Individually Aaron and I wanted to kill the bishop, and I'm not exaggerating. I kept hearing voices tell me, "Kill him. Kill him." At one point I remember the bishop gave me a cross and asked what I wanted to do with it.

"Beat the shit out of Nick with it," I responded. I wasn't even joking. The rage in me was fierce. I remember someone (I assume the bishop) giving me holy water, and it tasted like crap. That's a sure sign that I was in trouble because malnutrition and dehydration is the main cause of death during possession. The demonic entity does not allow the host body to be sustained and rejects all food and water.

Thankfully my judgment prevailed and I was able to get a hold of myself, but on the way back to the hotel, I wanted to fight. I didn't care who, I just wanted to fight.

People will laugh and scoff at us for this, but let them. I don't care if you're a believer or not. It happened. I know it's real. I would tell the nonbelievers to go to Bobby Mackey's themselves and see what it feels like, but that would be irresponsible. That's like telling them to look over the edge of the Empire State Building and then pushing them.

A Word of Warning

Places like Poveglia, Italy, and especially Bobby Mackey's, contain truly evil entities and are not starter investigations for people wanting to get into paranormal investigation. They're more like graduate-level research and should be left alone if you're inexperienced at this. These are the types of spirits who should not be approached by novices and even I have a hard time dealing with them. They want to hurt you. They want to traumatize you and if you walk into places like these with a cross, a vial of holy water, an attitude of invincibility, and a camcorder, you may regret it forever. By no means should anyone who wants to begin a career in paranormal investigation go to one of these places before they've developed the necessary experience and knowledge on how to deal with them. If you choose to ignore this warning, then you're on your own.

I believe the demonic entities that exist in Bobby Mackey's Music World could have been invited there by some very dumb (or hateful) humans. It's known to have been a place for satanic rituals in the past, which could have opened a portal for the infestation inside. After our final investigation at Mackey's Bishop Long completed a ritual there and the paranormal activity subsided. But now I hear people are returning and inviting the demons back in, which is dangerous.

Let's look at this place from a different angle. Remember my theory about the Villisca Axe Murder House having an evil entity that possessed a man and used him to kill eight people? Mackey's could be the same situation times ten. There have been so many documented attacks and murders that I have to believe something compels people to act in a way they normally wouldn't once they get inside. I know it happened to me, so I can only conclude that evil lurks in the crevices of Mackey's, waiting to pounce on an unknowing victim and take control of them. In my case I was fortunate enough to have someone with me who recognized the signs of possession and the knowledge of how to stop it.

Before I started on this journey, I wasn't terribly religious. I was baptized as a Catholic, but church only meant one thing to me—cookies after the service. But as my investigations go on over the years and my encounters with spirits and demons persist, I believe in God and pray like my life depends on it, especially before entering certain establishments. It's a by-product of looking a demon in the face and having a BFO (Blinding Flash of the Obvious) that heaven and hell undoubtedly exist. It's not just faith for me, but practical application too. I've seen the forces of God at work so I believe in them completely now.

For many people this is an uncomfortable topic. To believe in heaven you also have to accept the concept of hell and to believe in guardian angels, you have to accept the notion of nefarious demons as well. You really can't believe in one without the other. There has to be a yin to every yang, which means for every good spirit wandering the Earth there is probably an evil one that balances it out, kind of like the good Jedi and Sith Lords of *Star Wars* who balance out The Force.

If you're reading this book, then you're at least a little bit of a believer in the afterlife and can accept the notion that the spirits of the dead may be roaming the Earth. So convincing people that ghosts exist is not a huge stretch, but convincing them that angels and demons also exist is a whole new bag of squid. Believing in demons is an admission that there are servants of hell and forces of darkness out there. Evil challenges our core beliefs in religion and forces people to admit there is not just a heaven and hell, but a judgment day and an almighty power that chooses which one we go to.

No one wants to think about eternal damnation and the dire consequences of our actions (I can tell you that I had a hard time accepting it), but moments like these when a profound evil is undeniably present force us to confront this possibility. I don't like hanging out at the crossroads where religion and the paranormal meet, but it's almost unavoidable. Now that I have personally encountered good and evil spirits, I believe that there is a heaven and hell.

After three investigations at Bobby Mackey's where all kinds of unexplained evil and creepiness happened, there's one question that still bothers me. Why hasn't anything happened to Bobby himself? Like Red Roberts at the Goldfield Hotel, in all the years that he's owned the place, Bobby Mackey has never been attacked except for a piece of ceiling that fell on him after he decided to tear the property down and rebuild on an adjacent lot (that lot was then rendered useless by a mysterious fissure six inches wide by sixty feet deep that appeared out of nowhere just as Mackey was about to develop the land).

Incredibly, Bobby is actually a nonbeliever in the paranormal! To this day he says he does not believe in any of the bad things that have happened there, even after being sued by a patron for a demon attack. I think he's in demonic denial or is a puppet for the infestation and may have even been predestined to be the building's owner. Is it coincidence that he was born just down the railroad tracks from the building? Is it coincidence that his name is Robert Randall Mackey and the crooner killed in the place was Robert Randall? Is it coincidence that he knew the blueprint of the building before he ever stepped foot in it? Before Bobby converted it, it was an abandoned slaughterhouse that no one went near. Then he renovated it and brought in fresh meat for the demons that Carl Lawson released when he opened the well. Bobby Mackey's reminds me of the bar "Titty Twister" in the movie *From Dusk till Dawn*, where the owner is allowed to live by the vampires who have nested there. He has some sort of strange agreement between himself and the otherworldly forces that makes him untouchable. If our nightmares came true, the world would be filled with despair and darkness—and Bobby Mackey's would be the gates of hell.

The Demon Lair of Sin City

Just when I think I've seen it all, something new jumps out and grabs me or I have a realization that opens up a whole new bag of craziness. Bobby Mackey's has a profound hold on me, but I never realized just how deep it was until I spent a few days investigating an old mansion in my hometown of Las Vegas. This place holds either a spirit, a group of spirits, or maybe even a lair of demons that seems to have some sort of trans-demonic communication with the ones at Bobby Mackey's. You heard right—a demonic cell phone network between Las Vegas and Kentucky.

Nestled inside a gated community of ridiculously huge mansions on the outskirts of the city, there is an old estate that may have had a "killing room" as one of its central features (imagine what that does to the property value). It was reportedly used by an organized crime family in the 1980s to torture and kill their enemies in seclusion and now is infested by a malicious entity or possibly even a group of them.

Today it's a gutted and lonely shell of its former self, but during the years that the last owner lived there, he was nearly driven insane by the continuous attacks on him, his family, and even his dog. Women were taunted by disembodied, perverted voices, men were choked by an unseen force, and a near-possession was even reported.

I know evil lurks there, but the interesting question is what kind of evil? Better yet, how many evil entities are there? The experiences we had there crossed the lines between defined demons. The activity in this mansion was so inconsistent and fell into so many categories that it was (and still is) very hard to classify. Entities there have carried out demon-style attacks, thrown objects like a poltergeist, and preyed on women like an incubus. It was ripe with paranormal activity and showed characteristics of so many types of hauntings that I'm still not sure what to make of the place. I like to keep an open mind, so there's a possibility that this mansion is infested by a group of evil spirits, all of whom are struggling for control of the space. Now *that* would be a den of evil like no other.

Did you Know? We may have given the spirits at this mansion a jolt of energy prior to our investigation. Just before lockdown, our equipment went dead and our batteries all drained. And I'm not talking about a few D-cell batteries. We had two huge batteries that could power a small town, and both of them went dead before we even started. If spirits need energy to manifest then is it possible that we gave the evil spirits there a jumpstart?

But this place affected me on a personal level before I even set foot in it. Two nights before the investigation I had a dream I was at this particular mansion and I was standing next to a demonic being that was attacking people in the house. No matter how much they screamed, he kept doing it, but the weird part is that it left me alone. Not only that, it seemed to smirk at me like I was its sidekick and it was teaching me the ropes. In the dream, it wanted me to witness what it was doing and did not do any harm to me, and no matter how hard I tried, I couldn't do anything to prevent it. It was like we were cool with each other and had an unspoken bond.

A few days later I interviewed a man who lived at the Vegas mansion. He told me about being attacked by an unseen force in the house and how he was in a state of oppression afterward, as if the dark entity had gotten inside him and was struggling for control of his mind and body. He had violence in him that he never had before. Then he said something that made my blood run cold. "I felt like this entity and I clicked and we were cool with each other." That freaked me out. Not just a little, but a lot.

Two nights later we were investigating this mansion, which was chock full of ghoulies and activity, when I heard something that shook me to the core—"Three Blind Mice." It was being hummed the exact same way the demon at Mackey's had done it. On top of that, we captured an EVP of a disembodied voice mimicking my voice—the same way they had at Mackey's!

This was something way beyond anything I'd encountered. The EVPs I might be able to dismiss as coincidence, but probably not since I also caught one saying my name at Goldfield and the Ancient Ram Inn, but the humming of "Three Blind Mice" is just out of this world spooky. It's the most profound thing I have ever encountered because it hits me on a personal level. It's as if a demon or network of them are toying with me at these locations, which would indicate that they either have the ability to transport themselves or communicate with each other. Either way, they know how to find me and know where I will be, which is disturbing.

I think I have had some sort of demon attached to me since the first time I set foot in Bobby Mackey's. I think it sang the same song at Mackey's as it did in the Vegas mansion to let me know that it was there and that I could not get away from it. I think it mimics my voice to taunt me. And I think it's possessive of me to the point that it will scare away the women I date, but leave me alone. Some people claim to have a guardian angel. Do I have a guardian demon?

So You Want to Date Me?

"I want to hang out with you." I hear this statement all the time, but to be honest, no you don't. A lot of weird stuff has happened in my house to girls I have dated. I don't mind when it happens to me because I know how to deal with it, but when a spirit or a demon follows me home and attacks a guest, it really gets on my nerves. So if you were hoping to be invited over to my home for a barbeque or to hang out in my dungeon (yes, I have one) then I hate to say it, but it's not happening. I rarely have people over—not even close friends—because these are the things that can happen to them:

- A friend saw a ghost of a guy sitting in a chair in the middle of the night.
- A container of Palmolive soap hovered over a sink.
- A friend's cell phone levitated off a table and was thrown to the ground.
- My washing machine lid raising by itself and slammed shut.
- Rosary beads were ripped off a friend's neck and found in a room down the hallway and behind a closed door (that one was really creepy).
- Footsteps run up my stairs all the time. When you're going down the stairs and the spirit runs up, it can be very frightening.

- Voices tell my friends "leave!" and "get out of here."
- The padlock in my dungeon rattled by itself, scaring a friend.
- A cold breeze once hit me and several other people very hard and filled us with a feeling like we should leave.
- A friend felt that she was attacked in my kitchen. An unseen force played tug of war with her purse so she ran out of the house screaming and speaking in another language. True story.

You would think with all these things happening in my house that I would call someone to get rid of them, but I'm the paranormal expert here. I'm the one who helps others deal with their own paranormal activity, so it's just up to me to deal with it. However, I've had to cleanse the house with a priest three times due to oppression and thoughts of extreme violence. That doesn't exactly raise the resale value of the property.

It's not easy to stand your ground and face something you fear, especially when your body is frantically trying to decide between its instinctual fight-or-flight modes. When others run away from ghosts and scary places, I run toward them. Sometimes I don't know why, but I wouldn't have it any other way.

SECTION

VI

The Science

Is paranormal investigation really a science? Yes. Yes it is. I don't consider myself a scientist, but I would not be doing my job if I did not educate myself and stay on top of the latest theories surrounding our field of research. And what we do is just that—scientific research. I feel that it's important for anyone who wants to be a paranormal investigator to know what the prevailing theories in our field are, so together we can strive to either prove or disprove them. Comparing findings is a big part of advancing science and our field will not progress until we do so. How else will we be taken seriously if we do not have a common goal to work toward? Without boring you into a coma I will describe the difference between traditional and paranormal science, outline the major theories on life after death, and introduce you to the man who revolutionized science, Thomas Kuhn.

The Difference between Traditional Science and Paranormal Investigation

Paranormal investigation has been labeled a pseudoscience and discredited as fantasy by traditional scientists for decades. Most traditional scientists believe that paranormal researchers read crystal balls, hold hands in a circle, or conjure up false spirits through cheap parlor tricks with smoke and mirrors at carnivals for profit. Can you feel the love between the two fields?

Traditional science is anything but flawless. At some point in history, science tried to convince us that the world was flat, the world was the center of the universe, and that tobacco was not harmful. It's not that traditional science is full of idiots, but that their conclusions were based on incomplete information. I feel that both traditional scientists and paranormal investigators seek to find answers to the same questions and can compliment each other through comparative research. There are phenomena in this world that we cannot explain and it doesn't matter which side of the aisle you're on—believer or skeptic—we all want the same thing: the truth. I really hope we all can work together to find these answers in the future.

Unfortunately the disdain of the traditional scientists toward our field and the attitude that it's not a credible, natural science always blocks that cooperation. Too often paranormal research is viewed as a profiteering venture executed by the Miss Cleo's of the world who prey on the vulnerabilities of the weak. The core of traditional science's derision of the paranormal field is that it's filled with amateurs armed only with off-the-shelf equipment who do not adhere to the "scientific method" of research, which has been shaped and reshaped over the course of human history.

The scientific method is their bible. It's based on gathering observable, empirical, and measurable data subject to specific principles of reasoning. A scientific method consists of the collection of data through observation and experimentation, and the formulation and testing of hypotheses. Experimental studies are then established and executed to test the hypotheses, which must be repeatable to dependably predict future results.

The scientific method generally consists of characterizations (observations, definitions, and measurements of the subject of inquiry), hypotheses (theoretical, hypothetical explanations of observations and measurements of the subject), predictions (reasoning including logical deduction from the hypothesis or theory), and experiments that test everything.

Confused? Think about this—in 1738 Dutchman Daniel Bernoulli observed that water traveling through air caused a change in air pressure (ever see a shower curtain get drawn inward when you turn the water on?). He replicated this phenomenon in a laboratory environment and came up with the Bernoulli principle, which simply states that an increase in the speed of water traveling over a surface causes a decrease in pressure. Since water and air have roughly the same physical properties, the Bernoulli principle can be applied to the air flowing over an airfoil (a wing) and used to calculate the amount of lift applied to the foil. Bernoulli proved that air moving across the top of an airfoil travels faster than the air moving across the bottom. Therefore there is less pressure on top of the wing than there is underneath it and the wing lifts, causing flight.

There's more to it than that, but you get the point. Bernoulli observed a phenomenon, formulated a hypothesis to explain it, and set up experiments to gather observable, measurable data to verify or deny his reasoning, and then made the data available to the world for discussion. He followed a linear pattern that generally consisted of the following:

Define the question
Gather information and resources (observe)
Form a hypothesis
Perform an experiment and collect data
Analyze the data
Interpret the data and draw conclusions
Publish the results
Retest

Unfortunately, not everyone in the paranormal research field follows this process, and in fact it's filled with amateurs who simply crawl into a dark place with a digital recorder and ask questions, hoping for a response. Some of us do our best to follow the scientific method and seek answers the same way a traditional scientist would seek to explain natural phenomena, but there are major differences between the natural sciences and paranormal research that make our field unique.

1. The scientific method relies on repeatable experimentation to verify or deny data. Spirits of the departed are intelligent beings that don't always display a predictable pattern of behavior. They come and go at their leisure and have always proven to be elusive and inconsistent, maybe because they are frequently unaware of their state (deceased) and environment (the location and year).

There are several theories that can explain residual hauntings, but intelligent hauntings are different. They consist of the spirit of a deceased person who retained its identity and intelligence. Many times these intelligent hauntings will respond to questions of a personal nature when provoked, but they are rarely consistent and never predictable, so it's very difficult to show a repeatable pattern of behavior.

Paranormal activity cannot be replicated in a laboratory environment and therefore cannot be studied as closely as a natural science, like chemistry or biology. So the inability to replicate the phenomena makes verification and categorization of paranormal events very difficult and erodes the credibility of the science. After all, if we could summon spirits of the departed consistently and reliably in order to study them, there would be a whole new market in trans-dimensional communications.

2. Emotions frequently contaminate the data. Physicist and Nobel laureate Werner Heisenberg said, "What we observe is not nature itself but nature exposed to our method of questioning." Scientific inquiry must be unbiased to generate objective and reliable data. Since paranormal researchers generally believe in the afterlife already (especially when investigating the spirit of a departed loved one), they are frequently not as objective as they should be. Too many researchers have already reached a conclusion before they start an investigation and do their best to skew their findings in the direction of that conclusion.

It's not in keeping with the scientific model to investigate a purportedly haunted location with the intent to prove that ghosts exist. The paranormal researcher should remain neutral and unbiased throughout the investigation and let the data prove a definitive conclusion, whether that's the one they wanted or not. They should walk into an investigation thinking, "I will document what happens and then examine the data for conclusions."

I always debunk anything that shows the slightest hint of doubt and toss away evidence that can be explained through

natural forces. I try to maintain a skeptical approach to the paranormal, despite having multiple personal encounters with apparitions. I'm very wary of stating a location is truly haunted and
try to re-create situations to determine if natural, explainable
forces could be at work. It's one of the greatest challenges of
this field because we deal with emotions, both within ourselves
and the subjects that we study.

3. Paranormal phenomena do not always adhere to the
known laws of physics, which may be the crux of the matter—we need to reengineer our understanding of physics and
the ways of the universe. It's very possible that we're trying to
understand forces that aren't bound by gravity, space, or time,
and may in fact exist in a different plane or dimension. That
hypothesis requires a paradigm shift in our understanding of
physics and presents a fundamental problem—how do we measure and test the paranormal when the building blocks of the
universe are in question?

4. When experimentation is complete, researchers are expected to document and share their data and methodology so
they are available for careful scrutiny by other scientists. This
allows other researchers the chance to verify results by attempting to reproduce them and allows statistical measures of the
reliability of these data to be established. This is called "full
disclosure" and is an area that the paranormal field is lacking
in. Currently there is no repository of paranormal data or body
of evidence that researchers can turn to for comparing data.
Television shows and websites that document paranormal activity are really our only outlet. The drawback to not having a
database is that researchers cannot identify patterns of activity
and therefore can't derive theories or explanations of the para-

normal.

For example, it's widely accepted that paranormal activity increases around areas of high EMF. But why? If we had a database to compare EMF readings of every paranormal investigation, we could identify patterns and when cross-referenced against temperature readings, solar activity, moon phases, proximity to water, and other data, paranormal activity might even be predicted. Now lets add another layer—the surrounding materials of the haunting. It's widely believed that water and limestone heighten paranormal activity, hence the large number of haunted lighthouses and military forts. Now if we compare our previous data with the number of places built of limestone or in close proximity to water, we can start to form hypotheses to explain the phenomenon. A lack of a central database is hurting the research. We can't identify patterns and correlations. There's no consortium on the findings. There's no great library of paranormal evidence.

I see parallels in the places I go. The Ancient Ram Inn and Bobby Mackey's Music Hall are very similar. Kells Irish Pub and Moon River Brewing Company are similar. There are patterns in these places that have to be connected and explored. If we could do that, we might be able to predict when and where hauntings will take place.

5. Some paranormal activity can be justifiably explained as a cognitive action. "It's all in your mind," as some would say. And sometimes it is, as I will explain soon. The human brain is one of the frontiers that we still do not fully understand, and there are certainly phenomena that can be explained as tricks of the mind. Apparitions moving out of the corner of the eye are especially open to skepticism because it's been proven that objects on a person's periphery can seem to move when they're not.

Simply saying, "I saw a spirit and I know what I saw," isn't enough and does nothing to advance the field of paranormal research. Empirical, observable evidence has to be gathered. Skeptics frequently use the "cognitive function" defense to explain away paranormal activity, so multiple electronic recording devices (video and audio) are a must when conducting paranormal research to limit the margin of error. We'll look more at this later in the chapter.

There's also the question of money that holds paranormal research back. There is little to no profit in creating a center for paranormal research and only by creating entertainment shows out of investigations can researchers continue to have funds to carry out their work. Until paranormal investigators can demonstrate the practical value of their research to the public they will continue to be on the fringe and not receive real funding to advance the science. Ironically the paranormal was once a well-funded field with interest from prestigious universities and the federal government. But it was an immature science that still had to find its value, which it is doing now.

Multiverse Theory

While I am convinced that ghosts wander among the living, I don't want to close off the possibilities that their existence is due to a law of nature that we simply don't understand yet. I think paranormal activity could be the evidence quantum physics needs to prove their theories and in turn their theories could help prove spirits exist and an afterlife waits for all of us. Of course both fields have huge obstacles to overcome, especially in the way of tangible evidence, but together we may be able to solve some of the mysteries of the universe.

Bobby Mackey's is an evil place and I'm convinced that some sort of portal through time and space is held within its walls. As I mentioned earlier, I returned to Bobby Mackey's in 2010 for a private investigation with about fifty people. Nick caught a voice on his digital recorder, and when he played it back, we realized that the voice was mine. I had not uttered those words, "Hey guys. Be careful," any time in the recent past. A short while later, our paranormal friend, Tara Bohren, heard the voice of her daughter on the digital recorder.

So what could it have been? First off, the voice captured that evening was not audible with normal human hearing. It was captured on something we call a "shack hack" and recorded on a digital recorder. It's a device that continually scans all AM or FM frequencies to provide constant white noise to communicate on. Theoretically it also gives them snippets of words from the radio to grab a hold of and manipulate into their own words. In essence it provides a blank canvas for ghosts to paint on.

I will admit that the shack hack is controversial and sometimes picks up interference and stray radio transmissions, but these are never more than blips of sound with no substance. To ask a question and get an answer (or two) indicates an intelligent being is responding and you have not merely captured a stray radio transmission. Also when you put the recordings on a spectrograph and look at the waveform, it's possible to see how fast the frequencies are being scanned. It scans fourteen frequencies per second. At that rate it's impossible to make out a phrase, sentence, or even a word spoken by a human being broadcast over any regular radio frequency. It's like taking an old car radio and spinning the dial as fast as possible. All you hear is garbled blurbs, and yet we captured the same voice speaking a full sentence for several seconds. MY voice.

Since I had not been conducting any investigating upstairs that evening and I had no equipment that could transmit a signal, I made the assumption that this recording was not made that evening. I was also fairly certain it was not from the past (we would later compare the phrase through old recordings to see if I had uttered it during a previous investigation, and I had not).

As I already mentioned, my initial attempt to explain this is to go to the source—that the messages were from demons trying to make us angry or cause us pain. But there's another possible explanation that requires you to open your mind and take the parking break off your perception of the things you think you understand, like time and space. It's called quantum mechanics.

It's a fascinating science that's similar to ours in the need to accept new laws of physics, yet quantum mechanics is an accepted field of study while ours remains muddled in disbelief. I am by no means a quantum physicist, but I believe that some of their theories and research provide possible explanations of paranormal activity as natural processes. I think this event in the basement of Bobby Mackey's could be a good example of the multiverse theory.

The multiverse is a hypothetical set of multiple possible universes that together comprise everything that exists: the entirety of space, time, matter, and energy as well as the physical laws and constants that describe them. Multiverses might sound like something from a comic book (and I've read a lot of them) but the theory has gained traction in cosmology, physics, astronomy, philosophy, psychology, and fiction. They are referred to as "alternative universes," "quantum universes," and "parallel dimensions." It's basically a model that predicts that we are just one of an infinite number of worlds, all of which have copies of ourselves going about their lives in a nearly identical pattern to our own.

Proof of the existence of parallel dimensions can be found in physics and cosmology. We know there are stars with enough mass to collapse in on themselves, forming what we call black holes. Within a black hole, it's theorized that there is a point called a "singularity" where all physical laws may cease to exist. Time, space, gravity, electromagnetism, and light become unpredictable and one or all of these forces may not even be present. Without one or more of these basic forces, a new dimension forms that does not conform to the laws of physics as we know them. It's a parallel universe. When looked at this way, the possibility that we are just one of an infinite number of parallel universes is feasible.

Assuming there are parallel universes, let's add to that Einstein's theory of relativity, which taught us that time travel forward is possible, but time travel backward is not. However, time travel sideways into parallel dimensions (which could be a second or two behind us) is an intriguing possibility. As David Deutsch said in his 1997 book, *The Fabric of Reality*, "this would require a path between the two universes that is hardwired into the structure of the multiverse. Whether such paths exist or not is an unresolved empirical question."

Letting your mind go for a minute, it's possible that the recording of my voice could have been from a parallel dimension that exists merely seconds ahead of our own. In that universe, I discovered something and called it to the attention of my fellow investigators. At the same time, Tara Bohren's daughter, whom she decided to bring to the event in this parallel universe, asked for help. It sounds weird, but according to some of the most brilliant minds we have, it's entirely possible.

Black Holes and the Paranormal

The field of physics has debated these sorts of scenarios and possibilities for decades now. At the heart of their disagreement is the question of whether or not information can be destroyed. For a very long time the field of physics believed information (such as your memories) could not be destroyed. But Stephen Hawking challenged that and said black holes simply vanish over time, which means that basic information can be destroyed. That theory drew a line in the sand between those who agreed and those who said that information is eternal and is never lost.

Both sides use black holes as the focus of their theories because the laws of physics that we have formed over hundreds of years now completely break down in black holes. If we can figure out what truly happens around black holes, then we can unlock a lot of other secrets of the universe, including the paranormal.

The puzzle of whether or not information can be destroyed has a huge impact on the paranormal because if the traditional physicists are correct, then your soul does not vanish when you die, but instead becomes a part of the universe. That also leaves the door open for the possibility of pulling the elements of the soul back together briefly, which is what we call a manifestation. So some of the most brilliant and respected minds in the world of physics have actually given us reason to believe that it is scientifically possible for ghosts to exist, though not in the traditional sense of heaven and hell, demons and angels, Yankees and Red Sox. This is a more scientific approach, and while I lean more toward the spiritual side of the paranormal, I like to keep an open mind to what science thinks.

Let's look at the work of Doctor Stuart Hammeroff and

British mathematical physicist Sir Roger Penrose. They came up with a theory based on years of work in both medicine and physics. Hammeroff and Penrose showed a connection between the human brain and the fabric of the universe that goes like this: The brain is made up of neurons and microtubules that determine the architecture of the cells in the mind. They're like onboard computers for the brain that allow it to function as a quantum computer (which is very different from traditional computers). The traditional view of the brain is that activity causes neurons to fire (thoughts) and then cause connected neurons to fire to send signals around the brain like dominoes. It's called a traceable path, which is similar to how a conventional computer works.

However, Hammeroff and Penrose showed how activity in one part of the brain can cause activity in a completely unconnected part of the brain. It's a connection made by unseen microscopic components that they call entanglements, or a nonlocality connection. A change in one set of microtubules can cause a change in another set that is not even connected.

So if we take that information and apply it to a bigger stage, it's possible that every speck of the universe is connected and can contain quantum information. So microtubules can connect and entangle not only with the brain, but also with every part of the universe. It's possible that the whole brain can exist in the universe at large. This also implies that the soul is not constructed of just neurons, but the very fabric of the universe itself.

When the heart stops and blood flow ceases and the body's microtubules lose their quantum state, the information contained in the body becomes part of the universe. It is not destroyed. Hammeroff and Penrose showed that information and energy can exist outside the body as a soul in the universe. To be fair, they never meant their theory to apply to the paranormal. I made that connection.

Time Rivers and Relativity

Does time travel in a straight line? Most of us say yes, but there are some who say that time is not at all a straight line. Many quantum physicists agree that time is not linear and is actually a three-dimensional force that wanders and meanders around the universe following a pattern that we have not figured out yet. We classify time as a straight line because that's the only way our brains can comprehend it, but think about this— do you see any straight lines in nature? Rivers flow down the path of least resistance and trees grow in various directions to maximize their exposure to sunlight. Time could be the same. Einstein theorized that time is another dimension, woven together with space to form a fabric that is distorted by matter, which makes it anything but a straight line.

I agree with this theory and think time and space both flow in a random pattern on all three dimensions, which makes it possible that it can double back and overlap on itself. At these points where it either overlaps or comes close to overlapping is where it's possible for the space between the past, the present, and the future to be thin, which makes it possible to open a window on the past or the future. Gaining physical access to that window has theoretical issues, but capturing stray communications between times is certainly possible.

How does this affect the paranormal? I believe these windows are where we find residual hauntings. We think of residual hauntings as a loop of the same event in time happening over and over again like a broken record. It could be that these are spots on the time-space continuum where time flows from a defined source and overlaps the stationary moment. The basement of the Birdcage Theater is a good example. Thousands of people have reported hearing the same poker game playing out in the basement of the theater. It could be that this is really a "hotspot" in the flow of time where the fabric of space and time is very weak between the past and present.

There's another aspect of time to consider. Though most of us think of time as being constant, it's really not, unless you are a machine. Newton defined time as constant and precise, but Einstein proved him wrong. Einstein proved that, for humans, time is relative to the situation people find themselves in.

Think of this example: There are four people in a car driving from Washington, D.C., to South Florida for a Disney World vacation. The father (who is driving) has a clear perception of time and distance because he's watching the mile markers go by and his odometer slowly get higher. Time is constant to him. The mother in the passenger seat reads a book and has no concept of how far they've gone or what time it is, so to her, time is going by quickly. The son in the back seat is playing video games and is having so much fun that he does not want the trip to end. To him, time is going too fast. Meanwhile the daughter has to pee, so every second of the journey is agonizing and therefore very slow. All four of them have completely different perceptions of time.

For a teenager who's fawning over a new boyfriend or girlfriend and can't wait to see that person in school on Monday, the weekend sucks and goes by very slowly. For an adult, when was the last time you couldn't wait for a weekend to end? It's rare. Adults crave that space in between the working days and don't want it to end. Every Monday you can hear "that weekend went by too fast" echo through the halls of corporate America.

It's been proven that when the human brain thinks it is in danger, it can speed up its processing ability so that each second seems longer than normal. This is so it can determine what is happening and find a solution to the danger it faces. How many times have you heard someone say, "It seemed like time stood still," referring to a catastrophic event like a car crash?

The point here is that time is relative to the situation and the observer. It may be constant to an unbiased timepiece, but to those of us with brains, it's a flexible, constantly altering force of the universe and may be one of the reasons we experience residual hauntings.

Attachment Theory

Attachment theory is the belief that a spirit becomes attracted in some way to a living human and begins to coexist with (or even within) that person. It is believed these spirits find something comforting about someone and attach themselves to the person. Living people who share a building with the spirit of a deceased person can develop a relationship, and the spirit becomes intertwined in the life of the living. This is what happened to me in Trenton, Michigan, when I met my first ghost and she made a point of screaming my name every night.

I was fortunate that the spirit in Michigan left me alone after a week, but some spirits attach themselves and won't leave until they're forced to. They'll follow you from place to place and even to your home, no matter how far away it is. At two different locations in Nevada—Virginia City and Goldfield—I've captured the same voice speaking to me, which leads me to believe that the ghosts of the Old Washoe and Goldfield have either attached themselves to me or know when I'm in town. After my first investigation in the Old Washoe Club in 2004, I had heard from many people that the ghosts there were calling my crew and me out by name. On several occasions paranormal investigators have captured threatening and scary EVP recordings that said things like, "Nick, Zak, they're coming, kill."

How does a ghost know that I'm coming to town? How does the same spirit travel 250 miles from Virginia City to Goldfield? Does this mean they are not trapped in buildings, as we commonly believe, but choose to reside there because it's more comforting than wandering outside? Is there a network through which ghosts communicate with each other, or do they actually become part of our lives such that they can see and hear everything, including my calendar? Why do they become attracted to us and attach themselves in the first place?

I don't want to think the spirit world is so dark and confusing that ghosts need to anchor themselves to me or anyone else to in order to have hope. I don't want to think that the living is their beacon of light and that's why they can't let go of us. I believe instead that the spirits who attach themselves to the living are just confused and unaware of their surroundings and want someone to tell them what's going on. I think they're different from the good spirits like Anna Corbin and evil spirits like the ones in Bobby Mackey's. Those ghosts know who they are and have decided to stay here for one reason or another.

Whatever their motivation, spirits definitely become more active when you figure out what they're attached to. This is why trigger objects are so important. If you can figure out what entices the spirit and use that to lure them out, then you can make contact, but this is always a tricky situation. Attachments are more common among paranormal researchers because once we open the door and make it known that we're receptive, spirits seem to flock toward the light (the "light" in this case being the sensitive paranormal investigator, like me). It's a hazard of the job for sure and not one to be taken lightly. As I mentioned earlier, I'm convinced that spirits have followed me home from investigations and have even attacked my girlfriends in my home. I've had a few odd encounters with spirits who wanted to get rid of any woman that gets close to me.

Attachment theory can work in reverse too. I believe humans can also become attached to spirits and form a bond that they have difficulty breaking. Especially if the spirit is that of a loved one, humans can have a hard time tearing themselves away from a haunted building. The caretaker of the Ancient Ram Inn, Old Man Humphries, was probably under a state of oppression by the succubus that resided there or he would have moved years ago. He has an attachment not only to the spirit inside it, but the building itself, like Bobby Mackey has an attachment to his music hall.

The Burden of Proof

I'm always astounded when people ask me to prove that ghosts exist because I think in the opposite direction. I think the disbelievers need to prove that they *don't* exist. In a courtroom the burden of proof is on the accuser, not the defender, because everyone is innocent until proven guilty. When it comes to ghosts, the world is a nonbeliever and we have to prove them wrong, which I've always thought is backwards.

Normally the person making the extraordinary claim has the burden of proving to the experts and to the community at large that his or her belief has more validity than the one almost everyone else accepts. You have to make your opinion known, get a following, and then gather experts who agree so you can convince the majority to support your claim over the one that they have always supported.

This has happened many times in history. For millennia the accepted theory on the creation of the world was that God made it according to the Bible. But then Charles Darwin came along and convinced a majority of people that evolution and natural selection was how we got to where we are today. The burden of proof then switched to creationists, who found themselves in the minority for the first time and still are today. It is up to creationists to show why the theory of evolution is wrong and why creationism is right, and it is not up to evolutionists to defend evolution. The rationale for this is that mountains of evidence prove that evolution is a fact and until God rides a lightning bolt into St. Peter's Square and proves that he exists, creationism will be a minority belief.

There are people who believe that *Apollo 11* did not land on the moon in 1969, that the Holocaust never happened, and that Jim Morrison is still alive. But those people are such a small minority that they have to prove their case, since the overwhelming majority of humans believe the opposite. In other words, it is not enough to have evidence. You must convince others of the validity of your evidence. And when you are an outsider, this is the price you pay, regardless of whether you are right or wrong.

So are those of us who believe in the paranormal really the minority? A 2005 Gallup poll revealed that about three in four Americans claim at least one paranormal belief. The most popular belief is in extrasensory perception (41 percent) followed closely by belief in haunted houses (37 percent). Thirty-two percent believe that ghosts and/or the spirits of the dead can come back in certain places. When it comes to haunted houses, another 16 percent are unsure, bringing the total to 53 percent of Americans who either believe in ghosts or are unsure. That means those who do not believe (47 percent) are actually the minority. A special analysis of the data shows that even more Americans (73 percent) believe in at least one of ten listed paranormal activities.

We also have to remember that we're talking about forces no one understands just yet. If we have to prove to a group of experts that we are right, then what makes them qualified to say that we're wrong? How is a traditional chemist, biologist, or physicist qualified to say that there is no life after death? Have any of those disciplines proven that there is not? This is something the paranormal community will certainly struggle with for a long time.

Imprint Theory

Another paranormal theory is that energy left behind by a living person leaves an imprint on the universe the same way a paintbrush stroke leaves a mark on a canvas. We are all made of energy. We've established that. Now let's take it a step further and ask, "what it's the universe made of?" Imprint Theory states that everything in the universe is stored on a repository field the same way a computer chip stores data. This field is the very fabric of the universe and everything, including you and I, make an imprint of our energy on that field. As you read this book, you're making an imprint on the field. Therefore when a person encounters an apparition, he or she is actually getting a glimpse of that person on the field from another time. So the receiver of the paranormal energy is accessing another level of reality.

With the proper equipment we can see a similar phenomenon in the physical world. Place your hand on a table or a wall for thirty seconds and then pull it away. With the naked eye you won't see any physical remnant of the hand ever being there but with a thermal camera you can see the heat signature of the hand for ten to fifteen minutes until its energy dissipates. That's twenty to thirty times longer than the original placement of the hand. By that reasoning, a person who lived fifty years could have an energy imprint on the field for three thousand years.

But why does one noise, such as a scream or a voice, leave an imprint while others don't? Every scream, fit of laughter, and squeal of screeching tires doesn't resonate through time and echo for years to come, so what is special about the places where card games can still be heard, prison doors slam shut, and Slag still walks the yard?

Let's go back to the hand on the table. If the person leaving the imprint is upset, angry, or even in love, the heat signature that he leaves behind can last even longer. With emotions causing his blood to run faster, he will have a higher temperature in his hands and the impression will be deeper and last longer. So we can take that example and apply it toward the paranormal. Moments of extreme emotion can leave a longer and stronger impression on the universe than nonemotional ones.

I believe supercharged emotions have some sort of reaction with the universe that everyday life does not. We know that fear causes a release of adrenaline and gives the body the energy and strength it needs to overcome seemingly impossible obstacles (if you're into comic books—remember Dr. Bruce Banner and his work to release the body's inner strength that resulted in him becoming the Incredible Hulk?). When the human body is in peril and is afraid for its own survival, it becomes flooded with emotions that can leave a lasting impression on the very fabric of space and time. These emotional hotpots could validate imprint theory and be the places where paranormal activity occurs.

But imprint theory has a downside. It does a great job of explaining residual hauntings, but falls short of explaining intelligent hauntings. If paranormal activity is nothing more than the imprints of residual energies of life caught in a space-time loop, then how do you explain spirits who talk back to us and hold entire conversations? How do you explain the intelligent ghosts that know who they are and where they are? Imprint theory falls short of explaining a ghost that still has an identity.

Stone Tape and Water Tape Theory

Stone tape theory is almost the same as imprint theory. It says that certain natural materials can act like tape recordings and store the energies of the living. According to this theory, an event, usually one that involves a great deal of emotion, can somehow be captured in the stonework surrounding it and then replay like a tape recording in the future. The circumstances of release are usually inconsistent, meaning the stone lets go of the event at certain times and to certain people (and maybe even under certain weather conditions). For example an apparition of a miner running down a tunnel yelling "Cave in!" could be an event that was recorded by the rocks themselves. The energy from that event is stored and released at any given moment, resulting in a playback just like a tape recording. The spirit usually acts out the event with no regard to the living in its presence.

It's similar to imprint theory in that it explains residual hauntings, but differs in the material that stores the energy. Imprint theory states our energies are stored on the fabric of the universe, which is composed of time and space by a process that we have yet to figure out. Stone tape theory states that certain types of rock store the energy of significant emotional and traumatic events inside them.

This theory has some validity when you remember that iron oxide is the main component of audiotapes. Iron oxide is everywhere and the Earth's core is made mostly of iron and nickel. It has also been proven that certain crystals, like quartz, can retain information and are found almost everywhere and even within some rocks. Computer chips, used to store memory, are made from silicon, which is the second most abundant element on the planet next to oxygen and is found in almost every form of rock. So it's not a stretch to imagine that certain natural materials can store traumatic and emotional events. The puzzle we have to solve is why these materials record only moments of increased emotional states instead of everything that happens around them.

Of course this theory has challenges. To playback the re-cordings on audiotapes, you need a strong electromagnetic field, which is rarely present when residual hauntings play out (unless the spirits themselves are providing the EMF). With silicon-based computer chips, an integrated circuit and millions of transistors are embedded onto the chip, which are needed to recover the information stored on them. So it's not enough to say that past events are stored within rocks. There also has to be a mechanism to play them back. The real challenge is in finding that playback mechanism.

An example of this theory is the Hoosac Tunnel in western Massachusetts. The tunnel saw an incredible amount of tragedy as it was being bored out of the mountains in the nineteenth century. Over two hundred people died, many of them in vio-lent explosions and other mining accidents. The extreme emo-tions of those deaths could have been stored in the rocks of the tunnel, and today, it is very active with paranormal energy.

Old Fort Erie, where I caught the incredible shadow arm, is made of local Onondaga flint stone. Many haunted buildings (including the Trans-Allegheny Lunatic Asylum) are made of limestone, which is the base material for many haunted places and contains a great deal of silica.

It could be that it's not the stone itself, but the water mol-ecules inside the stone that record and store the energies of the living. Some research has shown that ordinary water molecules may be able to store memories and may even be able to pass on those memories to other water molecules. Water is a building block of life that has been shown to store the properties of other materials imprinted on it. Some homeopathic medicines under extreme agitation have been shown to "remember" the proper-ties of other chemicals even after those chemicals have been removed from the water (look up the work of immunologist

Professor Jacques Benveniste).

The theory here is that extreme emotional events can imprint themselves on nearby water molecules and then be released as the water evaporates. But if that were true then why would the memory stay for decades and even centuries after the event?

The answer (theoretically) is that the original molecules continually pass their imprinted memories to neighboring molecules. With each copy the memory becomes less clear and distinct the same way copying a videotape makes each copy fade. The water may also evaporate completely, which would cause the imprinted memories to disappear as well.

We know that water stored deep inside rocks takes a very long time to surface and evaporate, so it could be that the rocks retain the water and release them and the paranormal activity stored in them after a long period of time or after a disruptive event, like an earthquake or demolition. This water would retain a higher-quality copy of the original event memory, so the spirit or event may be seen clearer. If we go back to the Hoosac Tunnel example, every time a train rumbles through the tunnel, it could be releasing some of the trapped water inside it.

There might some truth to this, since ghosts fade over time. There are few, if any, spirits that can be attributed to cavemen or ancient civilizations like Rome or Greece. In fact, it's difficult to find any spirits that can be attributed to a living person more than five hundred years old. So why do they fade away? Could it be that the water in the building that they occupy is evaporating slowly and taking their memory with it?

If this is true, then maybe bodies of water (rivers, lakes, or moats) are storing the residual energy of the living as well. We know that EMF increases around water, so with a dedicated study, we may be able to show that the top 500 most haunted places in the world are on or near a body of water and therefore have a relationship to paranormal activity. Lighthouses on coastal areas are frequently full of activity. The Licking River flows within feet of Bobby Mackey's Music Hall. Castillo de San Marcos sits on a bay. The Hoosac Tunnel has a constant supply of water running through it from rain runoff above.

The human body is around 70 percent water and we know that we store memories, so it's possible that the water molecules inside our brains are the actual storage material for thoughts and memories instead of gray matter. The same may be true of nature—the rocks are the brains and the water inside them is the storage container for the memories of what happens around it. The Earth is made up primarily of rock and water, so it's not a far-fetched concept that these planetary building blocks record and store the events of the living organisms on it.

Think about this for a minute—any serious athlete or someone who is into physical fitness will swear that the body has muscle memory. When athletes work out they perform movements in a repetitive fashion that their muscles adapt to and get used to. It's why every bodybuilder will tell you that they vary their workouts often so they do not get stagnant. Muscles performing movements almost without being told is what they call muscle memory, even though we all know muscles do not contain brains and therefore have no ability to store memories. Musicians are the same way. They practice repetitive movements, like a guitar lick, a piano concerto, or a drum solo over and over until their fingers and arms can do it almost unconsciously. We know that muscles contain water, so it's possible that these water molecules can also store memories.

For us humans, certain moments can trigger either fond or painful memories. For me, the smell of salt air always makes me remember the days I would spend on the beaches of Florida as a teenager. For those who can't let go of high school, the sight of a Camaro can bring back the days of cruising down the main strip of their hometown. For some soldiers returning from combat, any loud bang can bring back dire situations when their lives were in danger and trigger an emotional response. The stone tape theory and water tape theory basically ask the question, why can't the natural elements of the world act the same way? Why can't rocks and water trap the energies of the things that happen around them and then release those memories under certain conditions?

Like imprint theory, this actually seems like a feasible explanation for residual hauntings, but it falls short of explaining the intelligent or evil entities I have encountered. Intelligent spirits are not mere memories that are released when the right conditions are present. They are independent, thinking spirits with their own identities and emotions. If we apply the stone tape and water tape theories to intelligent hauntings, then it's possible that the energies of some spirits are stored in rocks and water, but in a different level of consciousness. When the conditions are right and these spirits are released they manifest fully with their previous identities intact. This could be why full-bodied apparitions are so rare.

While we're talking about the relationship between spirits and water, I'm a believer in the theory that spirits can travel, but they can't cross water. For example, I felt fine after leaving the Poveglia Island investigation, which is rare. Usually I have bad dreams and it takes me a few days to get back to normal after an investigation. But after Poveglia, which is an island surrounded by a lagoon, I rebounded to my normal self very quickly. Not only that, but I slept very soundly in the days after the investigation. I really think the spirits trapped at Poveglia cannot cross the Venetian Lagoon, which is why they were not able to attach themselves to me.

𝔚eather 𝔓henomena 𝔗heory

Do people mistake natural weather phenomena as paranormal activity? On the other hand, can certain weather conditions actually increase spiritual activity? There are some who say rain, wind, relative humidity, temperature, barometric pressure, solar activity, infrasound, seismic activity, the geomagnetic field, and the phases of the moon can be mistaken for ghost activity. I think this happens sometimes, but I also believe that the right weather conditions can unlock paranormal activity and actually help make it happen.

British lecturer Vic Tandy's experience with infrasound is a great case study on the effects of weather and the paranormal and is something every investigator should know. One night Tandy was working in his laboratory in a medical manufacturing firm when he saw an apparition out of his peripheral vision. The next day he looked for what it was and discovered a very high field of infrasound in his office. Through experimentation with a colleague, Tandy made the connection that infrasound causes humans to have paranormal-like experiences.

Infrasound is sound that is lower than the normal limit of human hearing, usually quantified at 20 hertz or cycles per second. Infrasound sometimes results naturally from severe weather, surf, lee waves, avalanches, earthquakes, volcanoes, waterfalls, auroras, and lightning. It's believed that animals can detect infrasound and it is the reason they flee when severe weather, like a tsunami, is approaching.

So Vic Tandy saw a ghost in his lab and attributed it to infrasound playing tricks on his mind. Tandy went on to recreate his experience, and with the assistance of Dr. Tony Lawrence, he was able to publish his findings in the *Journal of the Society for Psychical Research.* Their research led them to conclude that infrasound at or around a frequency of 19 Hz has a range of physiological effects, including feelings of fear and shivering, sensations of disorientation and a feeling that a presence is in the room. Though this had been known for many years, Tandy and Lawrence were the first people to link it to ghostly sightings.

I respect their work, but I also want to throw my own theory out there. Instead of infrasound tricking the mind, I think it's possible for infrasound to make the spirit that is already there visible. I think it's possible that the presence of infrasound did not create a false apparition, but actually made it possible for one to be seen. I think there are spirits that can only be seen, heard, or felt under certain atmospheric conditions, and the presence of infrasound is one of those conditions. Just like infrared light can illuminate a spirit in the dark and give us a way to see something we normally would not, so can infrasound.

Think about this—the Aurora Borealis is a fantastic light show caused by a weather event near the Earth's magnetic poles. The lights, which are fascinating displays of color and light, occur when highly charged electrons from the solar wind interact with elements in the Earth's atmosphere, mostly oxygen and nitrogen. The solar winds (also called cosmic rays) become visible when they hit the magnetosphere, which is stronger near the poles.

But cosmic rays fall through the Earth's atmosphere all the time and at all locations, so why do they make light shows at the poles? The answer is the high level of magnetism there. Does this sound familiar? Does it sound like high levels of EMF that are present when apparitions are caught on film? All the elements are in place—highly charged particles, magnetism, and light. I think there's a similarity between the conditions that create the northern lights and the conditions that make apparitions visible.

Infrasound and resonance may play an even bigger role in the paranormal than EMF because everything vibrates, all the way down to the subatomic level, and everything has its own signature resonant frequencies. We are ultra sensitive to shifts and changes in not only our own natural resonant frequencies, but also those in our immediate environment. How many times have you gotten a "good vibe" off of someone you share things in common with?

Solar activity, geomagnetic storms, and the phases of the moon also affect ghost activity. We know that spirits needs energy to manifest, so it would stand to reason that when the air is charged with electricity (like after a lightning storm or during a solar flare) they have more opportunity to gather strength to be seen or heard.

There is a popular belief that paranormal activity increases just before, during, and just after a new moon. We know that the moon's phases affect the Earth's magnetosphere by blocking solar winds and allowing the field to stretch further into space. Since the moon is closest to the Earth during a full moon and furthest during a new moon, we know that the gravitational field of the planet and the magnetosphere are both in flux at this time. It's very possible that the atmosphere is supercharged with energy during this phase, which gives ghosts more ability to manifest.

Temperature also has an effect, both positively and negatively. During the winter months of October to February, electrostatic energy in the atmosphere is at its highest. High barometric pressure and high humidity also contribute to higher amounts of charged particles in the air. So if we combine these facts with the moon phase data, the best time for paranormal activity would be just after a storm and during a full moon in the winter. Any wonder why October 31 has always been regarded as the day all hell breaks loose?

Like tumblers in a combination lock, I believe certain weather phenomena can give paranormal activity strength. I think there are ideal combinations of temperature, humidity, barometric pressure, and moon phase that, when aligned, act like the Earth's EMF pump to give spirits more strength to manifest.

On the downside, temperature fluctuations can cause false paranormal activity too. Wood pops, pipes bump against each other, and buildings groan when the sun sets and the world gets a little colder after dusk. It's a basic law of physics—natural and manmade materials contract when the temperature drops. And when the temperature drops dramatically, these sounds happen in bunches and can be mistaken for spirits trying to make contact.

It almost pains me to admit that there are weather and natural phenomena like these that can cause false hauntings, but I also recognize that I have to be objective and acknowledge that these perfectly natural phenomena can affect the way we perceive the world around us. If I can walk into a room and immediately identify that there is a presence of extreme levels of EMF, infrasound, or some other natural culprit, then I don't even need to conduct an investigation.

This also highlights one of the drawbacks to paranormal research—we have no central repository for the data we collect. What if, for example, every photo of an apparition ever taken or every EVP of a disembodied voice ever recorded were available to the public in one place. Now imagine those pieces of evidence were tagged with all the weather data that were present when it was captured. We could compile and compare data and discover patterns of weather that could make paranormal activity more predictable.

Let's fantasize for a minute. Let's imagine we discovered that every class A EVP and every photo of a full-bodied apparition was captured between 55 and 80 degrees Fahrenheit when the relative humidity was above 74 percent, the barometric pressure was rising, and the moon was in a full or new state, and during the winter months. With this knowledge we could start predicting times when the strongest paranormal activity would occur and make a breakthrough in paranormal research.

It is my hope that more studies be done to establish the connection between the weather and paranormal activity. By making sightings more predictable, we can increase our chances of communication with spirits and start to really unlock the mysteries of the universe.

Cognitive Functions Theory

"It's all in your head," they say. And in some cases, they may be right, but in most cases, they are wrong. I stated earlier that the human body is the best detector of paranormal activity because of its long evolution and sensitivity to the world. I also think the brain is just as in tune with the environment and can accurately detect the presence of paranormal activity.

The human brain is what separates us from the rest of the animal kingdom. Our ability to think, reason, and feel has evolved and rocketed us to the top of the food chain in a relatively short time on the global timeline. But the brain is still a frontier that we do not fully understand yet, and it holds fascinating secrets waiting to be unlocked (it is estimated that we only understand about 25–30 percent of the brain). Many critics of the paranormal use this incomplete understanding of the brain as a defense and claim that paranormal activity is just a figment of our imaginations.

In humans the frontal lobes of the brain are where executive functions such as self-control, planning, reasoning, and thinking are located. They are enlarged for a mammal of our size, which is one of the reasons we are who we are. This is where all the important functions take place, so it is the area that we focus on when people start saying the paranormal is not real. It's the part of the mind where perceptions and realities overlap. I have read two studies that suggest the brain can be manipulated into believing that it is in the presence of an otherworldly being through the electrical stimulation of these lobes.

In the 1980s Dr. Michael Persinger stimulated the temporal lobes artificially with a weak magnetic field to see if he could induce a religious state in several subjects. He claimed that the field could produce the sensation of "an ethereal presence in the room" that some call a doppelganger. Dr. Susan Blackmore, psychologist and author of *The Meme Machine*, and Richard Dawkins, atheist and author of *The Blind Watchmaker*, visited Persinger and took part in his trials. Dawkins reported a range of minor effects (relaxation, sensations in his limbs, etc.), while Blackmore reported "one of the most extraordinary experiences" she had ever had. Persinger's trials were not conclusive, but all three agreed that stimulation of certain lobes in the brain can cause extraordinary sensations. These sensations can either be mistaken for spiritual activity or provide a closer connection to another dimension of reality.

The point is this—if the brain can be fooled into thinking it's in the presence of a spirit by electrical stimulation of certain lobes, then the big question we have to ask is "What is causing these stimulations?" If you are in a building and suddenly feel a spirit is nearby, but there is no source of electricity or EMF, then it's possible you are right. Even if your EMF detector is showing higher readings, you may still be right because ghosts give off EMF. On the other hand, if you run your EMF detector along some power lines and it's spiking much higher than normal, it could be that higher concentrations of EMF are making you feel afraid. We know that EMF interacts with the human mind in strange ways. It can cause feelings of nausea, disorientation, a presence in the room, and fear. And in the end, fear is the real factor that paranormal investigators have to be on the lookout for.

Fear is a big player when it comes to the paranormal for a couple of reasons. Some people have preconceived notions of what ghosts are and others simply fear the unknown. Fear is a product of knowing the possible consequences of your actions. If you don't know how badly you can get hurt doing something, then it's easy to be fearless. If you don't know that a plane can fall from the sky and kill everyone on board, then you are not afraid of flying. If you don't know that a demonic entity can painfully scratch you and follow you home, then you have no reason to fear it. I know better.

A little fear is healthy because it ensures that you don't get complacent, but in this business fear has to be controlled and eliminated as much as possible because it can get in the way of an effective investigation. As long as I've been doing this, I still get jumpy and frightened when things go bump in dark places. So I force myself to face my fears once the rush of being momentarily afraid and the pins and needles in my body have subsided. As you've seen in some of these chapters, I try to face my fears head on and defeat them.

Every human has a "fight-or-flight" instinct. We all get to a point where our body and mind tell us to either stand and fight or run away. There have been a few times I gave in and ran from a situation, but now that I'm more experienced I stand and fight. But that does not mean I still don't carry around a little fear. I just control it and stay focused on the task at hand.

I think anyone who does not fear the paranormal is simply a nonbeliever. Skeptics believe that there is nothing out there that can hurt them, so they are not scared. There are those who say they have no fear of the paranormal and will go anywhere at any time to find answers. I think these are really skeptics who do not understand or believe in the consequences of their actions.

There are many more interactions between the brain and the paranormal, but those could fill a book by themselves. Parapsychology is an area that we are nowhere close to understanding. There is a Parapsychology Association (PA) that was founded in 1957 at Duke University and is dedicated to the study of the paranormal and its interaction on the human brain. It's a great organization whose primary objective is to achieve a scientific understanding of "psi" and related phenomena. Since 1969, the PA has been an affiliated organization of the American Association for the Advancement of Science (AAAS).

The Ebb and Flow of Science

Here's what I really want people to know.

Many people assume that science itself is consistent, accurate, and trustworthy. In fact, science changes frequently and one of the leading proponents of scientific change was Thomas Kuhn. In 1962 Kuhn published *The Structure of Scientific Revolutions*, which challenged the evolution of scientific change. At the time there was a concept of how science ought to develop and a generally accepted theory of scientific progress, but Kuhn turned all of that upside down.

Basically it was believed that science developed by adding new truths to the existing database of old truths, or the increasing approximation of theories to the truth. Science was viewed as building blocks that are steadily added to a structure, like a Lego skyscraper, continually getting bigger and more comprehensive and eventually ending up with a law, such as the law of gravity. Occasionally science would have to correct a past error based on a new truth (such as the world is not flat after all) and start over. Progress might accelerate in the hands of a particular genius, like Albert Einstein, but progress itself was guaranteed by the steadfast and plodding scientific method, which I went over earlier.

Thomas Kuhn came along and dropped a bomb on everyone. He challenged this view and argued that science was not constant at all, but instead science underwent phases and had alternating "normal" and "revolutionary" (or "extraordinary") phases.

Normal science is like solving a puzzle. The scientist has a reasonable chance of success depending on his own ability and the degree to which the puzzle itself and its methods of solution have familiarity (meaning the puzzle-solver is not blazing a new trail and has some historical work to fall back on). Normal science is expected to accumulate a growing stock of solutions to the puzzles.

Revolutionary science is different. It is not cumulative and involves a revision of existing scientific belief or practice. Not all the achievements of the preceding period of normal science are preserved in a revolution, and indeed a later period of science may find itself without an explanation for a phenomenon that in an earlier period was held to be successfully explained.

So instead of using established blocks to build new knowledge upon, revolutionary science starts over from the ground level. Instead of continuing to build a skyscraper from the sixtieth floor, revolutionary science tears it down and starts over. This feature of scientific revolutions has become known as "Kuhn-loss."

Albert Einstein is a great example of a revolutionary phase in science. Until Einstein's time (1879–1955), the theories of Sir Isaac Newton ruled physics. Newton said that time is absolute and constant. It ticks away slowly, one second at a time. But Einstein overturned that notion. He argued that time is another dimension and is inseparable from space and that time is relative.

So in short:

In normal science, the theory is not questioned. In revolutionary science it is.

In normal science there is cumulative progress. In revolutionary science there is not.

In normal science change is incremental and gradual. In revolutionary science the change is total.

It's similar to setting a precedent in law. For example, in the case of *Brown vs. Topeka Board of Education* (1954) the United States Supreme Court made a landmark decision that declared state laws establishing separate public schools for black and white students were unconstitutional. From that moment forward it was illegal in *any* state at *any* time to segregate a school. That is the same as revolutionary science. In traditional science every state would have to establish its own segregation laws instead of using the new ruling as its own. In revolutionary science, the previous laws are all thrown out and are then rewritten.

According to Kuhn, revolutions are similar to normal science, but better, more positive, and give us an opportunity to open our minds to new answers, so they should be welcomed. Kuhn claimed that normal science can succeed in making progress only if there is a strong commitment by the relevant scientific community to their shared theoretical beliefs, values, instruments, techniques, and metaphysics. This constellation of shared commitments Kuhn at one point calls a "disciplinary matrix." For example, the field of chemistry has a database of truths (its disciplinary matrix) that it has compiled over the years, like the periodic table of elements. These truths should be shared with the other fields of science, like biology, physics, and astronomy.

But these matrices have anomalies. In every disciplinary matrix there is an unanswered puzzle that punches holes in the database and begs for a scientific revolution to answer it and revise the matrix. However, the decision to revise them is not always apparent or easy. According to Kuhn, a revision of a disciplinary matrix is not a decision that is rationally compelled, nor is the particular choice of revision rationally compelled, so the revolutionary phase is open to competition among differing ideas and rational disagreement about their relative merits. In short, people argue when they cannot agree on a truth.

This is the current position that paranormal researchers and traditional scientists find themselves in. The existence of paranormal energy challenges the disciplinary matrix of physics, chemistry, biology, astronomy, and psychology and presents an unexplainable anomaly to these fields. We are the hole in their thinking that they cannot explain, so they just turn a blind eye and ignore us. Paranormal activity doesn't adhere to the known laws of physics and challenges our beliefs on physical, spiritual, and religious levels, begging for a revolutionary phase in science.

The revolutionary search for a replacement paradigm is driven by the failure of the existing paradigm to solve certain important anomalies, in this case, the hundreds of thousands of reports of ghost sightings that cannot be explained by the existing disciplinary matrix. Any replacement paradigm had better solve the majority of those puzzles, or it will not be worth adopting in place of the existing paradigm.

In a nutshell, conservative scientists return to their base of knowledge instead of thinking innovatively and pressing the boundaries of revolutionary science. It's their comfort zone, so they have a tendency to shun paranormal research since it's outside that comfort zone. Paradigms and their theories are not questioned and not changed in normal science whereas they are questioned and are changed in revolutionary science.

So here's the big question: Does the continued existence of paranormal energy require a Kuhn-loss revolution?

The field of paranormal research is at the point that Kuhn described as an immature science, meaning it lacks consensus. There are differing schools of thought that lack a common database to develop a disciplinary matrix. Every investigation team out there has a unique thought process with differing procedures, theories, and biases, which makes it hard for the field to progress as a whole (for example, some schools believe that white noise provides spirits a platform to communicate while others think it does not). Even localized progress by a particular school is made difficult, since much intellectual energy is put into arguing over the fundamentals with other schools instead of developing a research tradition.

Success is what will unite the field. Let's say one paranormal investigation team makes a huge breakthrough or solves one of the theories above in a particularly impressive fashion. That success will draw people together and a widespread consensus will form around the new puzzle solvers. Imagine this—I prove beyond a shadow of a doubt that there's a connection between paranormal activity and the phases of the moon. Suddenly the paranormal world rallies around me and we get agreement on the processes and procedures of paranormal investigation.

That consensus would allow agreement on the fundamentals of research because a problem-solution will embody particular theories, procedures, and instrumentation, scientific language, metaphysics, and so forth. This will raise new problems with few solutions, but the new issues can be addressed and answered using the techniques agreed upon in the disciplinary matrix. THAT'S WHAT A SCIENTIFIC REVOLUTION IS.

As believers, skeptics, and critical thinkers, we must move beyond our emotional responses because by understanding how others have gone wrong and how science is subject to social control and cultural influences, we can improve our understanding of how the world works. It is for this reason that it is so important for us to understand the history of both science and pseudoscience. If we see the larger picture of how these movements evolve and figure out how their thinking went wrong, we won't make the same mistakes. The seventeenth-century Dutch philosopher Baruch Spinoza said it best: "I have made a ceaseless effort not to ridicule, not to bewail, not to scorn human actions, but to understand them."

SECTION
VII
The future

A question I get all the time is why do I continue to do this? After all the stuff I've been through—all the attacks, nightmares, sickness, and near-possessions—why is paranormal investigation something that I can't stop doing? Again, I like to look at things from a different angle. Instead of asking why I do this, I ask everyone else why they *don't* do it. Why doesn't everyone want to unlock the secrets of the universe and discover what's on the other side? Why isn't everyone interested to know what happens when we die?

I think there are people like me who like to explore the great unknown and just find different ways of doing it. Some explore space, the depths of the ocean, or race to the north and south poles on sleds. Some explore the inner workings of the brain. I explore the world in between worlds and try to chart a course for those who can't find their own way. I try to communicate with those who are lost, confused, and angry. And I try to find ways to protect those who are being victimized by evil. That's

253

my calling in life and what I will continue to do until I can't anymore.

So what does the future hold for the field of paranormal investigation as a whole? Here's what I think can (or will) happen:

I envision a day when EVPs can be used for law enforcement. As it is, police departments are generally skeptical of mediums, psychics, and ghost hunters even though we provide them with some great evidence. I think one day they will not only accept what we give them, but also make it a standard part of their police investigations.

Crazy? Well, how about this case—in 2007 a group was conducting a paranormal investigation in upstate New York when they captured several voices and a struggle on their digital recorders. It was clearly a fight between two people that sounded very desperate. It turned out that this particular room had been the location of a murder over a hundred years earlier, so it's possible that they captured residual energy from that moment. Let's imagine for a moment that a name had also come through on that EVP like "Stop Colonel Mustard!" Could that be used one day in a court of law? I think it will be.

Remember the Villisca Axe Murder House? While investigating it, we asked "who killed you?" and got a response that was "Andy," the name of one of the suspects in the killings that occurred there. Think about the implications of that. Is it possible that someday we can just ask a spirit who killed them? Will we be able to put a spirit on the witness stand in a court of law? Think about how dramatically crime would drop if everyone knew the spirits of the dead were watching and could identify them in a crime.

Of course for that to occur, the communication between the living and dead would have to be very good. Much better than it is now. If we could communicate flawlessly with spirits, then I also see a day when we actually help people cross over to their final destination. I think we'll be able to provide a spirit closure so they can be at peace and move on. That sounds like an ambitious goal, but just two hundred years ago medicine had no answers for polio, scurvy, chicken pox, and scarlet fever. Now they've been virtually eradicated by hard-working scientists and breakthrough immunizations. I like to believe in human ingenuity and creativity.

Visual means of making contact are getting better and better all the time. We're constantly trying new ways to capture apparitions like full-spectrum cameras, infrared cameras, and ultraviolet cameras. I don't think we'll ever find a spectrum of light that makes our world like the movie *Thirteen Ghosts*, where the characters had special glasses they wore that illuminated all the spirits around them, but we're getting closer to the time when they just can't hide from us anymore.

I think one day we will discover the best weather conditions that enhance paranormal activity and will be able to predict when it will happen. I stated earlier that I feel that the conditions have to be right to capture an ectoplasm mist or a truly paranormal being. The climate, humidity, moon phase, energy source, portals, and any other variables that we don't understand have to be in place and in the right sequence. It's like the numbers of a combination lock being in line, and once they are, we get a peek into the world beyond. When spirits have these variables in line and an energy source, they appear and disappear as quick as a flash of lightning in the desert, so discovering the conditions that allow them to manifest is a huge step toward communicating with them. I think one day we will.

It's one of the reasons paranormal science still involves a lot of guesswork—we still do not fully understand the conditions that need to be present for paranormal activity to occur. Once we do, though, we'll be able to accurately predict when spirits will appear and might even be able to use that small window to communicate with them. Imagine the things we will learn when that day comes.

I see a day when we have a central location to post all paranormal evidence so we can compare notes and detect patterns of paranormal activity. Almost every field of science has one, so for us to be taken seriously we need a central research center for everyone to bring their evidence, compare notes, and make new discoveries in the field. If we had a "Bagans Research Center" (hey, I can dream big) that held every EVP, recording, picture, video, etc, then we could make real breakthroughs in paranormal exploration.

I envision a day when some (not all) religious disagreements are put to rest by paranormal discovery. This is one thing that many will disagree with me on, but think about this—what does the existence or denial of the undead prove or disprove about religion? Let's say we accomplish our mission and find an undeniable piece (or group) of evidence that proves beyond a shadow of a doubt the existence of spirits that are either caught between the physical and spiritual world or who just refuse to stay quiet. What does that say about religion?

Some people will deny it no matter how good it is. Others will embrace it no matter how weak it is. Either way, proving that the afterlife exists can stop several religious disagreements and may ease some religious tensions. We can finally know what "moving on" really means.

In the future I want to plan an experiment where I bait a demon into finding me, kind of like a really weird version of hide-and-go-seek. I want to make it known where and when I will be to a demon and see if he shows up.

Crazy? Here's why. We humans have learned to communicate instantly with each other, so why can't they? I said before that I really believe the demons at Bobby Mackey's somehow communicated with the demons in Las Vegas and that's why they each taunted me in the same way. Is it possible that they're using our own technology against us? Do our cell phones and the Internet make it easy for these spirits to track and travel to where we are?

Think about this—if all the information flying around the world every second were gnats and you could see them, the skies would be blackened out completely. The terabytes of information flying through the air at any given time are immense. There are literally highways of energy and information surrounding us all the time. Remember earlier when we discussed how quantum physics believes completely unconnected places in the universe can actually share information with each other? Why can't demons learn to do the same?

That's what I think the future holds for our field. I've invited some of the best people in the paranormal field to comment on their visions of the future as well.

Gary Galka
Electrical Engineer and inventor of the Mel Meter.

I would not have acquired the awareness and growth in my life without experiencing the trauma of losing my daughter, Mel. Given this opportunity, I would love to focus and harness my thoughts on ways in which technology, like the RT-EVP, could help loved ones connect with each other and reach some level of acceptance and closure . . . thus allowing them to heal and move on with their lives. I can tell you that "knowing" that your child is safe and happy does help you to heal at an accelerated pace.

The TV shows, events and yes, even Zak's book have an important impact on many people. As people begin to understand and become more aware of the paranormal, they'll start to view life from the eyes of the soul. The applied technology created for paranormal investigators and researchers will eventually open the door to many ordinary people. It will provide them with the opportunity to view life and death from a completely new perspective that encourages acceptance, strengthens our spirituality, and enables them to reflect on our true reality and that which makes up our vast consciousness.

Mark and Debby Constantino
Paranormal investigators with 20 years of experience specializing in EVP (www.spirits-speak.com).

Mark Constantino—A few years ago, a young college woman was abducted from a friend's home and found dead in a field a few weeks later. Debby and I went to the site where the body was found and conducted an EVP session. Within minutes we received an EVP that said "Mom, Mom I'm drunk." We also recorded an EVP that said "Truck sold" when we asked about information on the person that committed this crime.

Days later we walked into the Reno police department and said, "You'll think we're crazy, but we believe we have some evidence in this case to share with you." We expected to be dismissed, but in the end we felt we had captured the voice of the victim and, as Debby saw it, if we didn't do the right thing with this EVP, we weren't worthy of receiving it. Whether they thought we were crazy or not wasn't important. Solving the crime was all that mattered. When the killer was eventually caught, it turned out that he had indeed sold his truck, just as the EVP suggested.

You would think law enforcement officials would want to receive help from paranormal investigators when solving crimes like this, and they have been turning to psychics for years. We would like to see a day when EVP will be utilized as well. Will this skepticism change in the future? I hope so, but I doubt it. We have to become a fully credible field and be taken seriously as a science first. That's not easy. I hope to see a day when paranormal evidence, like the EVPs we came up with, will be admissible in court. But first, guys like Bill Chappell and Gary Galka will have to continue creating new ways to better communicate with the other side—ways that make them more reliable and consistent. We have to get over the credibility issue that plagues paranormal research. We have to hone the science to make it part of a detective's kit. That might take more people coming forward as we did who aren't concerned about judgements people may have about them, and want to share their tangible evidence with local law enforcement. Cold cases are usually completely exhausted, so local police departments will take any break they can catch, even if it means listening to us.

But it shouldn't be that way. I want to see a day when a permanent paranormal investigator is on every police department's staff. Debby sees a day when the communication between this world and the next is so good that law enforcement just asks the dead spirit who committed the crime. I hope she's right, but I think that will take a long time and then there's always the matter of the courts. You can't call a dead person to the witness stand.

Another challenge we have to get over is consensus in the field. It's just not there right now. There are too many groups that are simply looking for their fifteen minutes of fame. It's a distraction and takes away from the credibility of the field. The procedures don't always translate to every paranormal group either. Antagonizing spirits works for some, like Zak, but not others. We're a long way away from paranormal unity. I agree with what Zak said earlier—if we had a database where people came together to compare their findings instead of staying secluded, we might be able to get over the credibility issue. Too many groups want to hold on to their evidence instead of sharing it. When you deal with people, you deal with their jealousy, and unfortunately that is, in part, what is holding this field back.

Debby Constantino—I would like to focus more of our time on helping find lost children. As well as grief management. There are so many kids who go missing and end up being found only when their body is identified by the police. I believe EVP is a powerful tool that can be used before something happens to them, not after.

I think when communication improves on our side, it will probably improve on the spirits' side as well. We were doing an EVP session once when Mark said, "You guys need to come through more clearly. We can't make out what you're saying." We then recorded an EVP that said "Reverse the polarity. Mark can't hear you." We always talk about ways to improve communication with the spirits, but I'm so curious to know what they're doing on their side to improve communication with us. Because I have no doubt, they are.

In the future I would like to see a day when EVP's are used to validate mediums/psychics. Unfortunately this is a field where anyone can label them self a psychic, and receive money for it. There are plenty of amazing psychics out there, who deserve compensation. There is no way to hone in on your path unless you do it on a full time basis. I see no problem with true mediums being compensated. There are others that are a disgrace to the field. I also look forward to a day when technology will hopefully make it possible for us to actually see the spirits we are communicating with. I hope this happens in our lifetime, as this will change everything.

Bishop James Long
Archbishop for the U.S. Old Catholic Church.

For ten years Bishop Long has been performing exorcisms and can tell you exactly how many he's done. "Twenty-four solemn rites of exorcism." And in all twenty-four cases he's "delivered" the entity from the host, which is the church's way of saying, "we banished that evil bitch." James has performed hundreds of lesser rituals of exorcism so it's his specialty and something he takes seriously after so much training and experience with demons. And that's exactly what scares him.

"Demonology has nothing to do with the paranormal," he says. "It's purely theological, and in fact exorcists and demonologists are not the same thing. I am concerned more and more that the information age will convince people they can do the things that have taken me nearly a decade to perfect. I am afraid people will claim to be demonologists because they read a book on it or see a rite being performed on YouTube. Then they'll try to perform their own exorcisms and get injured or even worse.

"People who are not trained in demonology and attempt to perform rituals that they have no business performing are playing with fire. If that trend continues, people are going to get hurt. When performing the solemn rite of exorcism, there's a real potential of the possessed person expiring. That right is reserved for an ordained clergyman and can be deadly if done wrong. People who have performed an exorcism incorrectly have been charged with manslaughter in the past, so in the future I hope this trend of amateurs performing exorcism stops."

John Zaffis
**Leading Paranormal Researcher
and Author and Host of *Haunted Collector.***

I think we're living the future now. The U.S. is looking at things differently than the rest of the world so we're blazing a trail for everyone else. Other countries are afraid to talk about the paranormal, but our TV shows open it up more and start the dialogue. But talk is just the start. I also want us to lead the way and prove what we talk about.

When you refer to our scientific base, we have EVPs, photos, videos, and all these other pieces of evidence, but what are we doing with it? Nothing. It's just sitting there. I want to see us do something with all of our evidence. We need correlation and cooperation. I wish paranormal investigators would intermingle and get along and share info more. I think they're too compartmentalized now.

It's a spiritual realm that we deal with, which makes it the hardest thing to prove. Scientists say we are not a real field of study because we can't get repeatability and our findings are not continuous. We need that if we ever want to be recognized as a real science. I want to see a day when we prove that these experiments are real so people look at it, and us, differently.

I agree that we need a dedicated research center, but it has to be removed from the paranormal community. It has to be staffed with people who are unbiased. Right now there is too much bickering internally. The paranormal community, in my estimation, is in chaos. It's a difficult field because everyone has their own ways and aren't too keen on sharing anything. If we had a college or a university who embraced our field then we could make progress. We need a structured environment where the PIs are not structured and the learning can take place. I hope to see that in the future.

My expertise is haunted items and attachment theory. I've spent thirty-seven years trying to determine how an ordinary item can hold on to spiritual energy. People and buildings can be possessed, so why not items like a typewriter or a vase? Everything is composed of energy—minerals, wood, metal, everything—so why can't paranormal energy be attached to everyday items?

The circumstances with haunted items are different than with people. You always have to ask "how did a spirit get associated with the item?" So many different theories apply. Spirits seem to find comfort in one item just as they did in life. Maybe a favorite item is the only thing that anchors them to the old world. It might have been a favorite chair that was not bequeathed to the right person and the spirit is upset about that. It might be a piece of jewelry that it coveted in life and still holds on to it. It's been proven that jewels and precious metals can store energy, so it's very common that jewelry is haunted.

The future of paranormal communication is exciting to think about. For hundreds of years, our communication technologies did not progress much. In the future, cell phones and iPods might be able to hold energy of the deceased. That makes communication devices an exciting prospect for communication with the dead. I've heard of cases of computers suddenly typing unexplained personal messages and cell phones coming to life when they shouldn't. Communications devices could be huge game changers for the paranormal in the future. Gary Galka is passionate about making new equipment to communicate with the departed sprits and is such a talented man. I'm excited that he or other talented individuals will achieve reliable communications and find the repeatability that our science community looks for.

Dave Schrader

Host of *Darkness Radio* and Coauthor of *The Other Side: A Teen's Guide to Ghost Hunting and the Paranormal.*

Some people criticize the current glut of paranormal TV shows and say that they're hurting the field as a whole. I disagree, but I also think there needs to be some change in the future. TV shows are good because they bring their subjects out into the open and make people talk about the paranormal openly instead of in a hush. Everyone has a story, and if they see others talking about it, then they will too instead of keeping to themselves and wondering if they're crazy.

Scientists watch the shows and try to prove us wrong, but that's fine too. As long as people are trying to get answers, then that's progress. Some of the best inventors and best advocates of paranormal activity started as skeptics and came into this field to get answers, only to be influenced by the results they were getting and dig deeper. That's exactly what we need more of.

The technology we have makes it easy for people to get to incidents quicker, and just about everyone has a phone with a camera now. That's good news because it means that a lot of people can be out there seeking answers that they don't get from churches, friends, science, and other outlets. The bad news is that a lot of these people keep their evidence to themselves because they want to be the ones to break it to the world. Nobody wants to share. No one wants to help each other out. Everyone thinks they can be an investigator and get their dramatic evidence on TV. Everyone wants the exclusive of investigating a location. Those people are in it for the wrong reasons, and until someone can step forward and say "this is an agreed-upon way of doing this," the field will have difficulty progressing.

This is the big drawback to all of the attention on the field and the improved technology—the huge number of hobbyists who really don't know what they're doing. I commend them for wanting to contribute, and there are amateurs who have come up with some great pieces of evidence. But it's the serious investigators who have been doing it a long time who will really make a difference and will force us to get better.

I think the day when we all collaborate is coming and hopefully Paranormal Challenge will help streamline things by getting teams to agree to accepted ways of doing things. That standardization is what we need. It seems the momentum and interest in the field is still going and there are great minds like Gary Galka and Bill Chappell (two former skeptics) who are inventing equipment to bridge the gap in technologies, so I don't see it slowing down. Paranormal interest is very cyclical. There are several phases in history where it's been very popular and then disappeared. Right now it's popular and people are seeking answers again and looking for something to cling to. Is there a plan to all of this? I think so.

Dr. Andrew Nichols
Director of the American Institute of Parapsychology.

The ghost hunting movement is not the same as parapsychology, although we are interested in some of the same topics. Hauntings and poltergeists are one aspect where the two fields cross over, but parapsychology is the study of "psi" (or psychic) experiences, such as telepathy, clairvoyance, remote viewing, psychokinesis, psychic healing, and precognition. These experiences seem to challenge contemporary conceptions of human nature and of the physical world. They appear to involve the transfer of information and the influence of physical systems independently of time and space, via mechanisms we cannot currently explain.

There are several areas of parapsychology, but applied and clinical parapsychology is the future of the field. In order for parapsychology and paranormal research to grow, there have to be practical applications. Researchers need to focus on developing ways for people to use the science and the findings of psychic research, which is currently a major drawback. Skepticism among scientists is also a big obstacle because we haven't been able to formulate testable theories on how these things work.

The good news is that psychology, which is mostly an accepted science, suffers from many of the same problems. Psychology has a dozen theories on how the mind works, most of them unproven, but it still expands. The dream of integrating mainstream psychology with parapsychology hasn't gone very far. We have dreams of parapsychology becoming an accepted branch of psychology, but that hasn't happened, and it's not likely to, so I think the only way our field will have a future is by carving it out ourselves.

We have to do what psychoanalysis did and just ignore the mainstream and establish our own theories and practices. Parapsychology has to develop its own models on how the mind works that are based just as much on experimental and empirical evidence as any other social science. We have to train our own parapsychologists, who can work with people who have had experiences that they can't explain. We have to stop worrying about what everyone else thinks and just move forward, and that means finding practical applications for what we do.

Within terms of law enforcement, I don't think police departments turn to psychics and mediums as a last resort, they're just the last resort that they'll admit to. A number of psychics work with the FBI and police, but law enforcement agencies don't like to admit it, which is a shame, but is understandable because of the stigma associated with it. We have to reduce that stigma through successful application. We have to show demonstrable results in sufficient quantity to overcome the resistance of the skeptics. There will always be some individuals who ridicule and deride the personal status of psychics to undermine the progress of this field until we become more credible.

Science is a tool, not a belief system for understanding the universe. The human mind has a transcendent function that provides us with awareness that we are interconnected in some unexplained way. Everyone seeks to understand the interaction between the human and the environment. That's what parapsychology is all about. Humans are part of the environment and at the deepest level of consciousness we are all connected. Most people sense this to be true.

The reality is that the public is on our side. Most people have admitted to having paranormal or psychic experiences and know it is real. At least 75 percent of the population has had at least one paranormal experience in their lifetime and while their experiences do not meet the rigors of scientific inquiry, they still believe.

The psychic experience is subjective and can't be recorded reliably by any means that we have today, but so are dreams, and we know those exist. Psychology studies dreams even though they're subjective, so why can't we study the interactions of the mind and the environment? As it is, dreams have to be relayed to the psychologist. They can't be directly recorded by any machine. The subject matter of parapsychology is similar; we try to tap into a different level of reality. We process psychic information all the time just as we process dream information all the time. Until science develops a device to record dreams, they have to be relayed subjectively by the dreamer the same way ghost experiences have to be relayed by the observer to the public.

Some ghost groups say they don't use psychics and sensitives, but that's a mistake. You can't have a paranormal experience without the human element, otherwise you're just talking about energy and energy can be a lot of different things. You have to have the psychic to relay the experience and the human mind to find the meaning in it. The best technology we have for detecting the paranormal is still the human mind, so I hope to see ghost groups and parapsychologists work together more to find the answers we all seek.

Joshua P. Warren
Paranormal Researcher and Author

Paranormal research is very much based in the field, and we need to transfer the data to lab experiments in a controlled environment to draw definite conclusions about the results. Everyone is focused on these experiences in the field, which is fun and important, but they do not hold up to science. We need to transfer our experiments and findings to a lab where we can show reliability and repeatability.

The greatest possible outcome of paranormal research is to develop a technology that can observe events that happened in the past. The idea is that we eventually develop a machine that functions like a pair of goggles that lets us see into the past, which I think is actually all around us now. Most ghostly phenomena seems to be the recreation of something that happened a long time ago. If we can understand how this works and adapt that knowledge to a technology that can allow us to see how that works, it will revolutionize *all* aspects of mankind. It will affect how we view ourselves and our personalities, and will have profound impacts on our privacy and who we are.

The big picture is this: Every event that has happened in

the past is still present. It is all around us and resonates at a frequency that we cannot transform into a visible frequency. But somehow the environment does it. The past and its energy are held in the present somehow by Mother Nature, which we humans are a part of. I believe the past is accessible at any moment in time. Past, present, and future could be happening at the exact same time. We are fairly certain that the environment can record past events. We just can't tap into that mechanism yet. If we could, then everything that has ever happened would be there to be observed. It's the ultimate goal of paranormal investigation.

Imprint theory is the first big step we should delve into. I believe it is correct in theorizing emotional events leave an imprint on the field of the universe. I've seen it. After that we should try to understand the conscious nature of life in general. Does something remain outside of the physical shell of what we live in (the traditional concept of ghosts)? The traditional viewpoint of humans containing a spirit that corresponds to the physical body is legitimate to me. Once we exist solely in that energy form away from our bodies, maybe we can interact with other spirits in a way that we don't understand yet. Therefore the next logical step is to determine whether or not humans can exist out of the body alone and in what capacity. We are made up of a physical body and an energy body and need to determine how the separation between the physical body and the energy body works.

Marie D. Jones
Author and Paranormal Explorer

The paranormal field should have no future. None at all. Allow me to explain.

My first major book *PSIence: How New Discoveries in*

Quantum Physics and New Science May Explain the Existence of Paranormal Phenomena, published several years ago, became the "bible" for many in the field seeking answers outside the box. Subsequent books, such as *The Resonance Key* written with Larry Flaxman, my partner in ParaExplorers, continued the exploration outside the box by focusing on potential mechanisms and causes for paranormal events, such as sound, acoustics, resonance and frequency, the power of belief and intention, the observer effect and consciousness, collective expectation, human physiology, and the role of the brain as receiver and perceiver.

What the hell did all this have to do with ghosts, ESP and aliens, many asked? Well, until we understood our own reality, we might never understand the "alternate" reality of the paranormal.

Instead, the focus remained on "ghost hunting," "UFO chasing," and "monster questing," all of which have their rightful and important place in putting the pieces of the paranormal puzzle together. But these activities focus only on effects—data such as EVP, photos, images, recordings, etc. So today, we have thousands of pieces of "effects" to look at, yet few causes for those effects. Let's be honest. Do we really need more EVP? More thermal images? More pictures of orbs and shadow figures? Don't we have enough by now to be able to extrapolate some hypotheses and theories from?

Without some brainpower focused on the causes, the effects become meaningless. The field cannot survive without attention to causes, despite all the great media interest it has merited and the growing number of groups out there hunting and collecting effects. And that means sitting down and coming up with theories, ideas, concepts, THOUGHTS . . . not quite as fun as a good ghost hunt, but necessary to complete the puzzle.

Where should we look for those causes? From quantum and theoretical physics, to seismology, biology, human physiology, and neurology (among other fields), the world of science provides necessary clues to the common denominators behind the origin and manifestation of paranormal phenomena. The study of human consciousness may also hold a key to understanding our own role in paranormal events. As the quantum world tells us, the presence of an "observer" is critical to the outcome of an experiment. What is the one common denominator present in any paranormal investigation or event? Us!

And when we begin to examine our own potential role (physiological and psychological) as either conduits or instigators (or both), of these events, we might finally "get it."

We once had no understanding of gravity, of the weak and strong nuclear forces, of DNA, of many things we now deem as factual. If we put our collective brainpower behind the causes and not just the effects, the paranormal will one day become obsolete. It will become normal.

We will finally get it.
No future required.

Acknowledgments

A book is not written overnight and rarely by one person alone. There are a lot of people who have played a part in getting me to where I am today.

I want to first thank my mother for believing in what I wanted to do with my life as it played a role in where I'm at today.

Thank you to my entire family for your awesome support in what I do: my dad, stepfather, and sister.

Thank you to my grandmother, Grace Gorno Bagans, for those awesome Italian dinners and comfort during some struggling times. . .will never forget the blackberry brandy!

I am so grateful to have two great friends, Aaron Goodwin and Nick Groff, who have accompanied me on most of my investigations.

I want to thank the BEST fans and supporters in the ENTIRE WORLD, The GAC Family.

I also am blessed to be surrounded in the paranormal community by great friends since the very beginning of my adventures, like Tara Bohren, Dave Schrader, Gary Galka, Mike Haberman, Billy Tolley, Zory, Bill Chappell, Bishop James Long, Mark and Debby Constantino.

And thanks to Kelly Crigger for always bugging the crap out of me to write more.